Har
Business
Review

ON

THE TESTS OF A LEADER

THE HARVARD BUSINESS REVIEW PAPERBACK SERIES

The series is designed to bring today's managers and professionals the fundamental information they need to stay competitive in a fast-moving world. From the preeminent thinkers whose work has defined an entire field to the rising stars who will redefine the way we think about business, here are the leading minds and landmark ideas that have established the *Harvard Business Review* as required reading for ambitious businesspeople in organizations around the globe.

Other books in the series:

Harvard Business Review Interviews with CEOs

Harvard Business Review on Advances in Strategy

Harvard Business Review on Appraising Employee Performance

Harvard Business Review on Becoming a High Performance Manager

Harvard Business Review on Brand Management

Harvard Business Review on Breakthrough Leadership

Harvard Business Review on Breakthrough Thinking

Harvard Business Review on Building Personal and Organizational Resilience

Harvard Business Review on Business and the Environment

Harvard Business Review on the Business Value of IT

Harvard Business Review on Change

Harvard Business Review on Compensation

Harvard Business Review on Corporate Ethics

Harvard Business Review on Corporate Governance

Harvard Business Review on Corporate Responsibility

Harvard Business Review on Corporate Strategy

Harvard Business Review on Crisis Management

Harvard Business Review on Culture and Change

Harvard Business Review on Customer Relationship Management

Other books in the series (continued):

Harvard Business Review on Decision Making
Harvard Business Review on Developing Leaders
Harvard Business Review on Doing Business in China
Harvard Business Review on Effective Communication
Harvard Business Review on Entrepreneurship
Harvard Business Review on Finding and Keeping the Best People
Harvard Business Review on the High-Performance Organization
Harvard Business Review on Innovation
Harvard Business Review on the Innovative Enterprise
Harvard Business Review on Knowledge Management
Harvard Business Review on Leadership
Harvard Business Review on Leadership at the Top
Harvard Business Review on Leadership in a Changed World
Harvard Business Review on Leading in Turbulent Times
Harvard Business Review on Leading Through Change
Harvard Business Review on Making Smarter Decisions
Harvard Business Review on Managing Diversity
Harvard Business Review on Managing High-Tech Industries
Harvard Business Review on Managing People
Harvard Business Review on Managing Projects
Harvard Business Review on Managing Uncertainty
Harvard Business Review on Managing the Value Chain
Harvard Business Review on Managing Your Career
Harvard Business Review on Managing Yourself
Harvard Business Review on Marketing
Harvard Business Review on Measuring Corporate Performance
Harvard Business Review on Mergers and Acquisitions
Harvard Business Review on the Mind of the Leader
Harvard Business Review on Motivating People

Other books in the series (continued):

Harvard Business Review on Negotiation and Conflict Resolution

Harvard Business Review on Nonprofits

Harvard Business Review on Organizational Learning

Harvard Business Review on Strategic Alliances

Harvard Business Review on Strategic Sales Management

Harvard Business Review on Strategies for Growth

Harvard Business Review on Supply-Chain Management

Harvard Business Review on Teams That Succeed

Harvard Business Review on Top-Line Growth

Harvard Business Review on Turnarounds

Harvard Business Review on Women in Business

Harvard Business Review on Work and Life Balance

Harvard Business Review

ON

THE TESTS OF A LEADER

A HARVARD BUSINESS REVIEW PAPERBACK

Printed in the United States of America
11 10 09 08 07 5 4 3 2 1

The *Harvard Business Review* articles in this collection are available as individual reprints. Discounts apply to quantity purchases. For information and ordering, please contact Customer Service, Harvard Business School Publishing, Boston, MA 02163. Telephone: (617) 783-7500 or (800) 988-0886, 8 A.M. to 6 P.M. Eastern Time, Monday through Friday. Fax: (617) 783-7555, 24 hours a day. E-mail: custserv@hbsp.harvard.edu.

Library of Congress Cataloging-in-Publication Data
Harvard business review on the tests of a leader.
p. cm. — (The Harvard business review paperback series)
Articles originally published in Harvard business review.
Includes index.
ISBN-13: 978-1-4221-1494-0 (pbk. : alk. paper)
ISBN-10: 1-4221-1494-5
1. Leadership. 2. Executive ability. 3. Management. I. Harvard business review.
HD57.7.H38736 2007
658.4′092—dc22 2007010706

Contents

Harvard Business Review

ON

THE TESTS OF A LEADER

Becoming the Boss

LINDA A. HILL

Executive Summary

EVEN FOR THE MOST GIFTED INDIVIDUALS, the process of becoming a leader is an arduous, albeit rewarding, journey of continuous learning and self-development. The initial test along the path is so fundamental that we often overlook it: becoming a boss for the first time. That's a shame, because the trials involved in this rite of passage have serious consequences for both the individual and the organization.

For a decade and a half, the author has studied people–particularly star performers–making major career transitions to management. As firms have become leaner and more dynamic, new managers have described a transition that gets more difficult all the time. But the transition is often harder than it need be because of managers' misconceptions about their role. Those who can acknowledge their misconceptions have a far greater chance of success.

For example, new managers typically assume that their position will give them the authority and freedom to do what they think is best. Instead, they find themselves enmeshed in a web of relationships with subordinates, bosses, peers, and others, all of whom make relentless and often conflicting demands. "You really are not in control of anything," says one new manager.

Another misconception is that new managers are responsible only for making sure that their operations run smoothly. But new managers also need to realize they are responsible for recommending and initiating changes–some of them in areas outside their purview–that will enhance their groups' performance.

Many new managers are reluctant to ask for help from their bosses. But when they do ask (often because of a looming crisis), they are relieved to find their superiors more tolerant of their questions and mistakes than they had expected.

EVEN FOR THE MOST GIFTED INDIVIDUALS, the process of becoming a leader is an arduous, albeit rewarding, journey of continuous learning and self-development. The initial test along the path is so fundamental that we often overlook it: becoming a boss for the first time. That's a shame, because the trials involved in this rite of passage have serious consequences for both the individual and the organization.

Executives are shaped irrevocably by their first management positions. Decades later, they recall those first months as transformational experiences that forged their leadership philosophies and styles in ways that may continue to haunt and hobble them throughout their careers. Organizations suffer considerable human and financial costs when a person who has been promoted because of strong individual performance and qualifications fails to adjust successfully to management responsibilities.

The failures aren't surprising, given the difficulty of the transition. Ask any new manager about the early days of being a boss—indeed, ask any senior executive to recall how he or she felt as a new manager. If you get an honest answer, you'll hear a tale of disorientation and, for some, overwhelming confusion. The new role didn't feel anything like it was supposed to. It felt too big for any one person to handle. And whatever its scope, it sure didn't seem to have anything to do with leadership.

In the words of one new branch manager at a securities firm: "Do you know how hard it is to be the boss when you are so out of control? It's hard to verbalize. It's the feeling you get when you have a child. On day X minus 1, you still don't have a child. On day X, all of a sudden you're a mother or a father and you're supposed to know everything there is to know about taking care of a kid."

Given the significance and difficulty of this first leadership test, it's surprising how little attention has been paid to the experiences of new managers and the challenges they face. The shelves are lined with books describing effective and successful leaders. But very few address the challenges of learning to lead, especially for the first-time manager.

For the past 15 years or so, I've studied people making major career transitions to management, focusing in particular on the star performer who is promoted to manager. My original ambition was to provide a forum for new managers to speak in their own words about what it means to learn to manage. I initially followed 19 new managers over the course of their first year in an effort to get a rare glimpse into their subjective experience: What did they find most difficult? What did they need to learn? How did they go about learning it? What resources did they rely upon to ease the transition and master their new assignments?

Since my original research, which I described in the first edition of *Becoming a Manager,* published in 1992, I've continued to study the personal transformation involved when someone becomes a boss. I've written case studies about new managers in a variety of functions and industries and have designed and led new-manager leadership programs for companies and not-for-profit organizations. As firms have become leaner and more dynamic—with different units working together to offer integrated products and services and with companies working with suppliers, customers, and competitors in an array of strategic alliances—new managers have described a transition that gets harder all the time.

Let me emphasize that the struggles these new managers face represent the norm, not the exception. These aren't impaired managers operating in dysfunctional organizations. They're ordinary people facing ordinary adjustment problems. The vast majority of them survive the transition and learn to function in their new role. But imagine how much more effective they would be if the transition were less traumatic.

To help new managers pass this first leadership test, we need to help them understand the essential nature of their role—what it truly means to be in charge. Most see themselves as managers and leaders; they use the rhetoric of leadership; they certainly feel the burdens of leadership. But they just don't get it.

Why Learning to Manage Is So Hard

One of the first things new managers discover is that their role, by definition a stretch assignment, is even more demanding than they'd anticipated. They are surprised to learn that the skills and methods required for success as an individual contributor and those required for success as a manager are starkly different—and that there is a gap between their current capabilities and the requirements of the new position.

In their prior jobs, success depended primarily on their personal expertise and actions. As managers, they are responsible for setting and implementing an agenda for a whole group, something for which their careers as individual performers haven't prepared them.

Take the case of Michael Jones, the new securities-firm branch manager I just mentioned. (The identities of individuals cited in this article have been disguised.) Michael had been a broker for 13 years and was a stellar producer, one of the most aggressive and innovative professionals in his region. At his company, new branch managers were generally promoted from the ranks on the basis of individual competence and achievements, so no one was surprised when the regional director asked him to consider a management career. Michael was confident he understood what it took to be an effective manager. In fact, on numerous occasions he had commented that if he had been in charge, he would have been willing and able to fix things and make life better in the branch. After a month in his new role, however, he was feeling moments of intense panic; it was harder than he had imagined to get his ideas implemented. He realized he had given up his "security blanket" and there was no turning back.

Michael's reaction, although a shock to him, isn't unusual. Learning to lead is a process of learning by doing. It can't be taught in a classroom. It is a craft primarily acquired through on-the-job experiences—especially adverse experiences in which the new manager, working beyond his current capabilities, proceeds by trial and error. Most star individual performers haven't made many mistakes, so this is new for them. Furthermore, few managers are aware, in the stressful, mistake-making moments, that they are learning. The learning occurs incrementally and gradually.

As this process slowly progresses—as the new manager unlearns a mind-set and habits that have served him over a highly successful early career—a new professional identity emerges. He internalizes new ways of thinking and being and discovers new ways of measuring success and deriving satisfaction from work. Not surprisingly, this kind of psychological adjustment is taxing. As one new manager notes, "I never knew a promotion could be so painful."

Painful—and stressful. New managers inevitably ponder two questions: "Will I like management?" and "Will I be good at management?" Of course, there are no immediate answers; they come only with experience. And these two questions are often accompanied by an even more unsettling one: "Who am I becoming?"

A New Manager's Misconceptions

Becoming a boss is difficult, but I don't want to paint an unrelentingly bleak picture. What I have found in my research is that the transition is often harder than it need be because of new managers' misconceptions about their role. Their ideas about what it means to be a manager hold some truth. But, because these notions are simplistic and incomplete, they create false expectations that individuals struggle to reconcile with the reality of managerial life. By acknowledging the following misconceptions—some of which rise almost to the level of myth in their near-universal acceptance—new managers have a far greater chance of success. (For a comparison of the misconceptions and the reality, see the exhibit "Why New Managers Don't Get It.")

Managers wield significant authority. When asked to describe their role, new managers typically focus on the rights and privileges that come with being the boss. They assume the position will give them more authority and, with that, more freedom and autonomy to do what they think is best for the organization. No longer, in the words of one, will they be "burdened by the unreasonable demands of others."

New managers nursing this assumption face a rude awakening. Instead of gaining new authority, those I have studied describe finding themselves hemmed in by interdependencies. Instead of feeling free, they feel constrained, especially if they were accustomed to the relative independence of a star performer. They are enmeshed in a web of relationships—not only with subordinates but also with bosses, peers, and others inside and outside the organization, all of whom make relentless and often conflicting demands on them. The resulting daily routine is pressured, hectic, and fragmented.

"The fact is that you really are not in control of anything," says one new manager. "The only time I am in control is when I shut my door, and then I feel I am not doing the job I'm supposed to be doing, which is being with the people." Another new manager observes: "It's humbling that someone who works for me could get me fired."

The people most likely to make a new manager's life miserable are those who don't fall under her formal authority: outside suppliers, for example, or managers in another division. Sally McDonald, a rising star at a chemical company, stepped into a product development

---

Why New Managers Don't Get It

Beginning managers often fail in their new role, at least initially, because they come to it with misconceptions or myths about what it means to be a boss. These myths, because they are simplistic and incomplete, lead new managers to neglect key leadership responsibilities.

	Myth	Reality
Defining characteristic of the new role:	**Authority** "Now I will have the freedom to implement my ideas."	**Interdependency** "It's humbling that someone who works for me could get me fired."
Source of power:	**Formal authority** "I will finally be on top of the ladder."	**"Everything but"** "Folks were wary, and you really had to earn it."
Desired outcome:	**Control** "I must get compliance from my subordinates."	**Commitment** "Compliance does not equal commitment."
Managerial focus:	**Managing one-on-one** "My role is to build relationships with individual subordinates."	**Leading the team** "I need to create a culture that will allow the group to fulfill its potential."
Key challenge:	**Keeping the operation in working order** "My job is to make sure the operation runs smoothly."	**Making changes that will make the team perform better** "I am responsible for initiating changes to enhance the group's performance."

position with high hopes, impeccable credentials as an individual performer, a deep appreciation for the company's culture—and even the supposed wisdom gained in a leadership development course. Three weeks later, she observed grimly: "Becoming a manager is not about becoming a boss. It's about becoming a hostage. There are many terrorists in this organization that want to kidnap me."

Until they give up the myth of authority for the reality of negotiating interdependencies, new managers will not be able to lead effectively. As we have seen, this goes beyond managing the team of direct reports and requires managing the context within which the team operates. Unless they identify and build effective relationships with the key people the team depends upon, the team will lack the resources necessary to do its job.

Even if new managers appreciate the importance of these relationships, they often ignore or neglect them and focus instead on what seems like the more immediate task of leading those closest to them: their subordinates. When they finally do accept their network-builder role, they often feel overwhelmed by its demands. Besides, negotiating with these other parties from a position of relative weakness—for that's often the plight of new managers at the bottom of the hierarchy—gets tiresome.

But the dividends of managing the interdependencies are great. While working in business development at a large U.S. media concern, Winona Finch developed a business plan for launching a Latin American edition of the company's U.S. teen magazine. When the project got tentative approval, Finch asked to manage it. She and her team faced a number of obstacles. International projects were not favored by top management, and before getting final funding, Finch would need to secure agreements with regional distributors representing 20% of the Latin American market—not an easy task for an untested publication competing for scarce newsstand space. To control costs, her venture would have to rely on the sales staff of the Spanish-language edition of the company's flagship women's magazine, people who were used to selling a very different kind of product.

Winona had served a stint as an acting manager two years before, so despite the morass of detail she had to deal with in setting up the new venture, she understood the importance of devoting time and attention to managing relationships with her superiors and peers. For example, she compiled biweekly executive notes from her department heads that she circulated to executives at headquarters. To enhance communication with the women's magazine, she initiated regular Latin American board meetings at which top worldwide executives from both the teen and women's publications could discuss regional strategy.

Her prior experience notwithstanding, she faced the typical stresses of a new manager: "It's like you are in final exams 365 days a year," she says. Still, the new edition was launched on schedule and exceeded its business plan forecasts.

Authority flows from the manager's position. Don't get me wrong: Despite the interdependencies that constrain them, new managers do wield some power. The problem is that most of them mistakenly believe their power is based on the formal authority that comes with their now lofty—well, relatively speaking—position in the hierarchy. This operating assumption leads many to adopt a hands-on, autocratic approach, not because they are eager to exercise their new power over people but because they believe it is the most effective way to produce results.

New managers soon learn, however, that when direct reports are told to do something, they don't necessarily respond. In fact, the more talented the subordinate, the less likely she is to simply follow orders. (Some new managers, when pressed, admit that they didn't always listen to their bosses either.)

After a few painful experiences, new managers come to the unsettling realization that the source of their power is, according to one, "everything but" formal authority. That is, authority emerges only as the manager establishes credibility with subordinates, peers, and superiors. "It took me three months to realize I had no effect on many of my people," recalls one manager I followed. "It was like I was talking to myself."

Many new managers are surprised by how difficult it is to earn people's respect and trust. They are shocked, and even insulted, that their expertise and track record don't speak for themselves. My research shows that many also aren't aware of the qualities that contribute to credibility.

They need to demonstrate their *character*—the intention to do the right thing. This is of particular importance to subordinates, who tend to analyze every statement and nonverbal gesture for signs of the new boss's motives. Such scrutiny can be unnerving. "I knew I was a good guy, and I kind of expected people to accept me immediately for what I was," says one new manager. "But folks were wary, and you really had to earn it."

They need to demonstrate their *competence*—knowing how to do the right thing. This can be problematic, because new managers initially feel the need to prove their technical knowledge and prowess, the foundations of their success as individual performers. But while evidence of technical competence is important in gaining subordinates' respect, it isn't ultimately the primary area of competence that direct reports are looking for.

When Peter Isenberg took over the management of a trading desk in a global investment bank, he oversaw a group of seasoned, senior traders. To establish his credibility, he adopted a hands-on approach, advising traders to close down particular positions or try different trading strategies. The traders pushed back, demanding to know the rationale for each directive. Things got uncomfortable. The traders' responses to their new boss's comments became prickly and terse. One day, Isenberg, who recognized his lack of knowledge about foreign markets, asked one of the senior people a simple question about pricing. The trader stopped what he was doing for several minutes to explain the issue and offered to discuss the matter further at the end of the day. "Once I stopped talking all the time and began to listen, people on the desk started to educate me about the job and, significantly, seemed to question my calls far less," Isenberg says.

The new manager's eagerness to show off his technical competence had undermined his credibility as a manager and leader. His eagerness to jump in and try to solve problems raised implicit questions about his managerial competence. In the traders' eyes, he was becoming a micromanager and a "control freak" who didn't deserve their respect.

Finally, new managers need to demonstrate their *influence*—the ability to deliver and execute the right thing. There is "nothing worse than working for a powerless boss," says a direct report of one new manager I studied. Gaining and wielding influence within the organization is particularly difficult because, as I have noted, new managers are the "little bosses" of the organization.

"I was on top of the world when I knew I was finally getting promoted," one new manager says. "I felt like I would be on the top of the ladder I had been climbing for years. But then I suddenly felt like I was at the bottom again—except this time it's not even clear what the rungs are and where I am climbing to."

Once again, we see a new manager fall into the trap of relying too heavily on his formal authority as his source of influence. Instead, he needs to build his influence by creating a web of strong, interdependent relationships, based on credibility and trust, throughout his team and the entire organization—one strand at a time.

Managers must control their direct reports. Most new managers, in part because of insecurity in an unfamiliar role, yearn for compliance from their subordinates. They fear that if they don't establish this early on, their direct reports will walk all over them. As a means of gaining this control, they often rely too much on their formal authority—a technique whose effectiveness is, as we have seen, questionable at best.

But even if they are able to achieve some measure of control, whether through formal authority or authority earned over time, they have achieved a false victory. Compliance does not equal commitment. If people aren't committed, they won't take the initiative. And if subordinates aren't taking the initiative, the manager can't delegate effectively. The direct reports won't take the calculated risks that lead to the continuous change and improvement required by today's turbulent business environment.

Winona Finch, who led the launch of the teen magazine in Latin America, knew she faced a business challenge that would require her team's total support. She had in fact been awarded the job in part because of her personal style, which her superiors hoped would compensate for her lack of experience in the Latin American market and in managing profit-and-loss responsibilities. In addition to being known as a clear thinker, she had a warm and personable way with people. During the project, she successfully leveraged these natural abilities in developing her leadership philosophy and style.

Instead of relying on formal authority to get what she wanted from her team, she exercised influence by creating a culture of inquiry. The result was an organization in which people felt empowered, committed, and accountable for fulfilling the company's vision. "Winona was easygoing and fun," a subordinate says. "But she would ask and ask and ask to get to the bottom of something. You would say something to her, she would say it back to you, and that way everyone was 100% clear on what we were talking about. Once she got the information and knew what you were doing, you had to be consistent. She would say, 'You told me X; why are you doing Y? I'm confused.' " Although she was demanding, she didn't demand that people do things her way. Her subordinates were committed to the team's goals because they were empowered, not ordered, to achieve them.

The more power managers are willing to share with subordinates in this way, the more influence they tend to command. When they lead in a manner that allows their people to take the initiative, they build their own credibility as managers.

Managers must focus on forging good individual relationships. Managing interdependencies and exercising informal authority derived from personal credibility require new managers to build trust, influence, and mutual expectations with a wide array of people. This is often achieved by establishing productive personal relationships. Ultimately, however, the new manager must figure out how to harness the power of a team. Simply focusing on one-on-one relationships with members of the team can undermine that process.

During their first year on the job, many new managers fail to recognize, much less address, their team-building responsibilities. Instead, they conceive of their people-management role as building the most effective relationships they can with each individual subordinate, erroneously equating the management of their team with managing the individuals on the team.

They attend primarily to individual performance and pay little or no attention to team culture and performance. They hardly ever rely on group forums for identifying and solving problems. Some spend too much time with a small number of trusted subordinates, often those who seem most supportive. New managers tend to handle issues, even those with teamwide implications, one-on-one. This leads them to make decisions based on unnecessarily limited information.

In his first week as a sales manager at a Texas software company, Roger Collins was asked by a subordinate for an assigned parking spot that had just become available. The salesman had been at the company for years, and Collins, wanting to get off to a good start with this veteran, said, "Sure, why not?" Within the hour, another salesman, a big moneymaker, stormed into Collins's office threatening to quit. It seems the shaded parking spot was coveted for pragmatic and symbolic reasons, and the beneficiary of Collins's casual gesture was widely viewed as incompetent. The manager's decision was unfathomable to the star.

Collins eventually solved what he regarded as a trivial management problem—"This is not the sort of thing I'm supposed to be worrying about," he said—but he began to recognize that every decision about individuals affected the team. He had been working on the assumption that if he could establish a good relationship with each person who reported to him, his whole team would function smoothly. What he learned was that supervising each individual was not the same as leading the team. In my research, I repeatedly hear new managers describe situations in which they made an exception for one subordinate—usually with the aim of creating a positive relationship with that person—but ended up regretting the action's unexpected negative consequences for the team. Grasping this notion can be especially difficult for up-and-comers who have been able to accomplish a great deal on their own.

When new managers focus solely on one-on-one relationships, they neglect a fundamental aspect of effective leadership: harnessing the collective power of the group to improve individual performance and commitment. By shaping team culture—the group's norms and values—a leader can unleash the problem-solving prowess of the diverse talents that make up the team.

Managers must ensure that things run smoothly. Like many managerial myths, this one is partly true but is misleading because it tells only some of the story. Making sure an operation is operating smoothly is an incredibly difficult task, requiring a manager to keep countless balls in the air at all times. Indeed, the complexity of maintaining the status quo can absorb all of a junior manager's time and energy.

But new managers also need to realize they are responsible for recommending and initiating changes that will enhance their groups' performance. Often—and it comes as a surprise to most—this means challenging organizational processes or structures that exist above and beyond their area of formal authority. Only when they understand this part of the job will they begin to address seriously their leadership responsibilities. (See the sidebar "Oh, One More Thing: Create the Conditions for Your Success" at the end of this article.)

In fact, most new managers see themselves as targets of organizational change initiatives, implementing with their groups the changes ordered from above. They don't see themselves as change agents. Hierarchical thinking and their fixation on the authority that comes with being the boss lead them to define their responsibilities too narrowly. Consequently, they tend to blame flawed systems, and the superiors directly responsible for those systems, for their teams' setbacks—and they tend to wait for other people to fix the problems.

But this represents a fundamental misunderstanding of their role within the organization. New managers need to generate changes, both within *and outside* their areas of responsibility, to ensure that their teams can succeed. They need to work to change the context in which their teams operate, ignoring their lack of formal authority.

This broader view benefits the organization as well as the new manager. Organizations must continually revitalize and transform themselves. They can meet these challenges only if they have cadres of effective leaders capable of both managing the complexity of the status quo and initiating change.

New Managers Aren't Alone

As they go through the daunting process of becoming a boss, new managers can gain a tremendous advantage by learning to recognize the misconceptions I've just outlined. But given the multilayered nature of their new responsibilities, they are still going to make mistakes as they try to put together the managerial puzzle—and making mistakes, no matter how important to the learning process, is no fun. They are going to feel pain as their professional identities are stretched and reshaped. As they struggle to learn a new role, they will often feel isolated.

Unfortunately, my research has shown that few new managers ask for help. This is in part the outcome of yet another misconception: The boss is supposed to have all the answers, so seeking help is a sure sign that a new manager is a "promotion mistake." Of course, seasoned managers know that no one has all the answers. The insights a manager does possess come over time, through experience. And, as countless studies show, it is easier to learn on the job if you can draw on the support and assistance of peers and superiors.

Another reason new managers don't seek help is that they perceive the dangers (sometimes more imagined than real) of forging developmental relationships. When you share your anxieties, mistakes, and shortcomings with peers in your part of the organization, there's a risk that the individuals will use that information against you. The same goes for sharing your problems with your superior. The inherent conflict between the roles of evaluator and developer is an age-old dilemma. So new managers need to be creative in finding support. For instance, they might seek out peers who are outside their region or function or in another organization altogether. The problem with bosses, while difficult to solve neatly, can be alleviated. And herein lies a lesson not only for new managers but for experienced bosses, as well.

The new manager avoids turning to her immediate superior for advice because she sees that person as a threat to, rather than an ally in, her development. Because she fears punishment for missteps and failures, she resists seeking the help that might prevent such mistakes, even when she's desperate for it. As one new manager reports:

"I know on one level that I should deal more with my manager because that is what he is there for. He's got the experience, and I probably owe it to him to go to him and tell him what's up. He would probably have some good advice. But it's not safe to share with him. He's an unknown quantity. If you ask too many questions, he may lose confidence in you and think things aren't going very well. He may see that you are a little bit out of control, and then you really have a tough job. Because he'll be down there lickety-split, asking lots of questions about what you are doing, and before you know it, he'll be involved right in the middle of it. That's a really uncomfortable situation. He's the last place I'd go for help."

Such fears are often justified. Many a new manager has regretted trying to establish a mentoring relationship with his boss. "I don't dare even ask a question that could be perceived as naive or stupid," says one. "Once I asked him a question and he made me feel like I was a kindergartner in the business. It was as if he had said, 'That was the dumbest thing I've ever seen. What on earth did you have in mind?' "

This is a tragically lost opportunity for the new manager, the boss, and the organization as a whole. It means that the new manager's boss loses a chance to influence the manager's initial conceptions and misconceptions of her new position and how she should approach it. The new manager loses the chance to draw on organizational assets—from financial resources to information about senior management's priorities—that the superior could best provide.

When a new manager can develop a good relationship with his boss, it can make all the difference in the world—though not necessarily in ways the new manager expects. My research suggests that eventually about half of new managers turn to their bosses for assistance, often because of a looming crisis. Many are relieved to find their superiors more tolerant of their questions and mistakes than they had expected. "He recognized that I was still in the learning mode and was more than willing to help in any way he could," recalls one new manager.

Sometimes, the most expert mentors can seem deceptively hands-off. One manager reports how she learned from an immediate superior: "She is demanding, but she enjoys a reputation for growing people and helping them, not throwing them to the wolves. I wasn't sure after the first 60 days, though. Everything was so hard and I was so frustrated, but she didn't offer to help. It was driving me nuts. When I asked her a question, she asked me a question. I got no answers. Then I saw what she wanted. I had to come in with some ideas about how I would handle the situation, and then she would talk about them with me. She would spend all the time in the world with me."

His experience vividly highlights why it's important for the bosses of new managers to understand—or simply recall—how difficult it is to step into a management role for the first time. Helping a new manager succeed doesn't benefit only that individual. Ensuring the new manager's success is also crucially important to the success of the entire organization.

Oh, One More Thing: Create the Conditions for Your Success

NEW MANAGERS OFTEN DISCOVER, belatedly, that they are expected to do more than just make sure their groups function smoothly today. They must also recommend and initiate changes that will help their groups do even better in the future.

A new marketing manager at a telecommunications company whom I'll call John Delhorne discovered that his predecessor had failed to make critical investments, so he tried on numerous occasions to convince his immediate superior to increase the marketing budget. He also presented a proposal to acquire a new information system that could allow his team to optimize its marketing initiatives. When he could not persuade his boss to release more money, he hunkered down and focused on changes within his team that would make it as productive as possible under the circumstances. This course seemed prudent, especially because his relationship with his boss, who was taking longer and longer to answer Delhorne's e-mails, was becoming strained.

When the service failed to meet certain targets, the CEO unceremoniously fired Delhorne because, Delhorne was told, he hadn't been proactive. The CEO chastised Delhorne for "sitting back and not asking for his help" in securing the funds needed to succeed in a critical new market. Delhorne, shocked and hurt, thought the CEO was being grossly unfair. Delhorne contended it wasn't his fault that the company's strategic-planning and budgeting procedures were flawed. The CEO's response: It was Delhorne's responsibility to create the conditions for his success.

Originally published in January 2007
Reprint R0701D; HBR OnPoint 1723

Courage as a Skill

KATHLEEN K. REARDON

Executive Summary

A DIVISION VICE PRESIDENT blows the whistle on corruption at the highest levels of his company. A young manager refuses to work on her boss's pet project because she fears it will discredit the organization. A CEO urges his board, despite push back from powerful, hostile members, to invest in environmentally sustainable technology. What is behind such high-risk, often courageous acts?

Courage in business, the author has found, seldom resembles the heroic impulsiveness that sometimes surfaces in life-or-death situations. Rather, it is a special kind of calculated risk taking, learned and refined over time. Taking an intelligent gamble requires an understanding of what she calls the "courage calculation": six discrete decision-making processes that make success more likely while averting rash or unproductive behavior. These include setting attainable goals, tipping the power balance in your favor, weighing risks against benefits, and developing contingency plans.

Goals may be organizational or personal. Tania Modic had both types in mind when, as a young bank manager, she overstepped her role by traveling to New York–on vacation time and on her own money–to revitalize some accounts that her senior colleagues had allowed to languish. Her high-risk maneuver benefited the bank and gained her a promotion.

Lieutenant General Claudia J. Kennedy weighed the risk and benefits before deciding to report a fellow officer who had plagiarized a research paper at a professional army school. In her difficult courage calculation, loyalty to army standards proved stronger than the potential discomfort and embarrassment of "snitching" on a fellow officer.

When the skills behind courageous decision making align with a personal, organizational, or societal philosophy, managers are empowered to make bold moves that lead to success for their companies and their careers.

A DIVISION VICE PRESIDENT blows the whistle on corruption at the highest levels of his company. A young manager refuses to work on her boss's pet project because she fears it will discredit the organization. A CEO urges his board, despite push back from powerful, hostile members, to make a serious investment in environmentally sustainable technology. Such things happen every day in firms around the world. What is behind these high-risk, often courageous acts?

The U.S. senator and onetime prisoner of war John McCain has defined courage as a brief, singular occurrence: "that rare moment of unity between conscience, fear, and action, when something deep within us strikes the flint of love, of honor, of duty, to make the spark that fires our resolve." This definition conjures up an image of the lone hero who—instinctively, spontaneously, and against all odds—suddenly takes charge and stands up for virtue.

Certainly, courage is sometimes a matter of life and death. Police officers and firefighters risked and lost their lives saving people on September 11, 2001; people dove into swirling waters to rescue strangers after a giant tsunami swept Indonesia in 2004. Yet in my 25 years of studying human behavior in organizations, I've discovered that courage in business seldom operates like this. Through interviews with more than 200 senior and midlevel managers who have acted courageously—whether on behalf of society, their companies, their colleagues, or their own careers—I've learned that this kind of courage is rarely impulsive. Nor does it emerge from nowhere.

In business, courageous action is really a special kind of calculated risk taking. People who become good leaders have a greater than average willingness to make bold moves, but they strengthen their chances of success—and avoid career suicide—through careful deliberation and preparation. Business courage is not so much a visionary leader's inborn characteristic as a skill acquired through decision-making processes that improve with practice. In other words, most great business leaders teach themselves to make high-risk decisions. They learn to do this well over a period of time, often decades.

Learning to take an intelligent gamble requires an understanding of what I call the "courage calculation": a method of making success more likely while avoiding rash, unproductive, or irrational behavior. Six discrete processes make up the courage calculation: setting primary and secondary goals; determining the importance of achieving them; tipping the power balance in your favor; weighing risks against benefits; selecting the proper time for action; and developing contingency plans.

Setting Goals

The first component of the courage calculation answers these questions: What does success look like in this high-risk situation? Is it obtainable? If my primary goal is organizational, does it defend or advance my company's or team's principles and values? If my primary goal is personal, does it derive solely from my career ambitions or also from a desire for my organization's or even society's greater good? If I can't meet my primary goal, what is my secondary goal?

Suppose a well-regarded coworker is about to be fired. He has been maligned, and the person who poisoned his well did so to clear his own path to promotion. Colleagues have been grumbling about this, but no one has stepped forward to counter the false accusations. The senior manager who will do the firing is a poor listener and tends to kill messengers. Given the politics, should you try to save your coworker? Would doing so advance both the firm's and your own goals, preferably without making the senior manager look inept?

Whether primary or secondary, your goals should be reasonably within reach, not pie-in-the-sky ambitions. A primary goal that serves the organization might be either to rescue a good employee or to prevent the senior manager from acting on faulty information. A secondary organizational goal might be to apprise the senior manager of a "rat" in the company's midst. A primary goal that serves you personally might be to receive some behind-the-scenes credit for helping the employee. A secondary personal goal might be to feel that you did something for the greater good.

Although the odds of success will be hard to estimate before the other decisions in the courage calculation have been made, it is possible at this stage to think about the likelihood of primary-goal achievement. The venture capitalist Tania Modic, for instance, managing partner of Western Investments Capital, took a big risk in her first job out of college, as the assistant marketing development officer at an international bank. Modic's fancy title had a catch: There was no marketing development officer for her to assist, and the work she was assigned was unchallenging. The ambitious Modic wanted to contribute to the bank's success and also to her own advancement. Having helped many people senior to her, she knew she had the skills to do their jobs. So, using vacation time and her own money, she traveled to New York, called on some accounts that her senior colleagues had allowed to languish, and revitalized them. When she returned, some high-placed noses were out of joint, but her courageous action gained the attention of senior management, and she was rewarded with praise and, later, a promotion.

Modic was not merely brash. She thought clearly about her goals and the circumstances surrounding her high-risk maneuver: the culture of the organization, her personal history and skills, and the points of view of others involved. Her primary goal was organizational—to revitalize the dead accounts—and she estimated her chances of achieving that goal at about 70%. Her secondary goal was personal—to raise her visibility—and she saw a 60% chance of succeeding at that. She estimated her chances of getting fired at about 50%—or higher if she failed to rescue the accounts. Modic decided that she could live with these odds: The upside for the bank was considerable, and for herself, she believed, even bad visibility was better than none. She took the plunge, and went on to an impressive career. Like many effective leaders, Modic succeeded by recognizing, early in her career, the advantages of careful risk calculation over impulsiveness.

Determining Your Goals' Importance

The second component of the courage calculation addresses these questions: Just how important is it that you achieve your goal or goals? If you don't do something about the current state of affairs, will your company suffer? Will your career be derailed? Will you be able to look at yourself in the mirror? Does the situation call for immediate, high-profile action or something more nuanced and less risky? Courage is not about squandering political capital on low-priority issues.

To distinguish such squandering from constructive risk, John Hallenborg, a Los Angeles–based senior entertainment manager, assigns importance at three levels. On the lowest rung of his risk-taking ladder are issues about which he does not feel strongly, though he may prefer a particular outcome and may say so in a low-risk situation. Middle-rung issues are those about which his opinion is strong but doesn't involve higher values; his feelings may change based on new information. At the top of the ladder are "spear in the sand" issues. He perceives these as resting on morals or values for which he is willing to take a stand and fight.

Spear-in-the-sand situations require that you weigh your belief in the cause against the risks involved. Such situations are rare: They occur when negotiation is difficult or impossible, open minds are hard to find, and doing nothing is simply not an option. Peter Rost, a physician, formerly with Pfizer, drove his spear into the sand when he broke ranks with his employer by calling for legislation allowing the import of lower-priced medicines from Canada and elsewhere—a practice the U.S. drug industry strongly opposes. He also put his job on the line in efforts to halt the sale of off-label drugs and the associated incentives for physicians. Rost did not take on the pharmaceutical industry lightly, and the move cost him his career. But his convictions were too strong to ignore. He left the industry and went on to write *The Whistleblower: Confessions of a Healthcare Hitman.*

Tipping the Power Balance

People often assume that power in corporations is a simple matter of position on the organization chart. In attempting to please those above them, many people choose never to take a stand. But in reality, even those in top management give power to anyone on whom they are dependent—whether for respect, advice, friendship, appreciation, or network affiliations. Seen this way, power is something over which we really do have considerable control. By establishing relationships with and influencing those around you, for example, you gain sway over people who otherwise hold sway over you. This gives you a broader base from which to make bold moves.

You can wisely form supportive power networks in advance, but building them takes time. In 1981 Jack Gallaway developed his power base as part of a courage calculation on behalf of Ramada. At the time, Gallaway was president of the Tropicana hotel and casino in Las Vegas, which Ramada owned. The company, having spent $340 million to construct its Atlantic City casino, was selling off hotels to make up for a 300% cost overrun. The last thing Ramada's board and top managers wanted to consider was any kind of expansion. But Gallaway believed that expansion in the booming Las Vegas market was critical.

When he approached Ramada's senior managers about adding another hotel tower to the Tropicana, they told him to stick to his knitting. "They wouldn't even give me the money to work on the concept designs," he recalls. He decided to see what he could do by leveraging his external network: He contacted an executive with Mardian, a Phoenix-based real estate developer. This was a clever move, because the powerful chairman of Ramada himself had previously passed on the executive's name.

Gallaway knew that Mardian was in the process of building a stadium in Las Vegas, and that the executive and other employees would need a place to stay while in town. So he made a trade: He provided Mardian's people with hotel rooms and transportation for a week in exchange for a complete set of concept drawings and an architectural model of a new Tropicana tower, worth more than $100,000. Mardian's senior managers knew this would give them the inside track if the hotel expansion was actually undertaken.

Gallaway's calculation paid off. When the Atlantic City operation opened in 1982, Ramada was again in the black, and Gallaway made his move. He presented Ramada's board with the drawings and the model, and the board approved the project. He knew that he could have been handed his head for going against the board's instructions, but he lowered the risks by tipping the power balance—working with someone he'd found through Ramada's chairman. Meanwhile, he proved himself a loyal "citizen" by keeping his operation's numbers up. By the time the company's financial crisis was over, Gallaway had secured an invaluable foothold in Las Vegas.

Weighing Risks and Benefits

This component of the courage calculation focuses on trade-offs. Who stands to win? Who stands to lose? What are the chances that your reputation will be tarnished beyond repair if you go forward? Will you lose respect or your job? Cause others to lose theirs? Delay your opportunity for promotion?

Lieutenant General Claudia J. Kennedy, the first female three-star general in the U.S. Army, went through a difficult risk-benefit assessment before reporting a fellow officer who had plagiarized a research paper at a professional army school. Kennedy weighed the negatives (discomfort and embarrassment for "snitching" on a fellow officer) against the positives (allegiance to the army's high standards for its future leaders, and adherence to her own ethics). The decision was difficult: An instinct for self-protection, loyalty to her colleagues and to the institution, and her personal integrity all contended within her. She considered speaking privately to the officer, but realized that he would react angrily and that, after all, it wasn't her job to manage him. In the end, she decided that her loyalty to army standards was paramount: "I . . . recognized that overlooking an ethical lapse was tantamount to participating in the event," she writes in her book *Generally Speaking.* She discreetly reported the incident; her reputation remained intact and her career thrived.

Other trade-offs deal with the quality of the action and the strategy involved. Are your goals better served if you act in a direct and forceful way or if you take an indirect approach? A story I call "Send Him a Rose" exemplifies the calculation required here. A division vice president who had a habit of enraging underlings stormed into the office of Rick Sanders (not his real name), the editor of an in-house corporate newspaper. The VP accused Sanders of not having checked his facts before printing a story about the VP's division. He ranted and raved, giving Sanders no chance to point out that the facts in question had come from the VP's own assistant.

At first Sanders wanted to send the executive a scathing e-mail. He knew that doing so would mean saying good-bye to his job. He was angry enough not to care, but he considered the costs to his division: The VP would probably refuse to work with Sanders's colleagues in the future, and their reputation with the CEO would be sullied. Sanders was far less willing to chance this. "If I reacted too strongly," he remembers thinking, "I'd run a big risk of hurting my team. Still, I felt I had to do something."

Sanders chose a judolike approach suggested by a colleague, who told him to "send the VP a rose" in the form of a disarmingly professional memo. The memo reminded the executive of the good relations their two departments had enjoyed over the years. Sanders said he regretted the inaccuracy but mentioned that the facts had been checked with the VP's assistant. He ended with a hope for positive collaboration in the future. The memo was not apologetic; rather, it was civil and to the point, and it invited a higher level of discourse—in essence, teaching the executive how to behave like one. After calculating the benefits of such a move, Sanders opted for what John F. Kennedy, in *Profiles in Courage,* described as a less glorified but nevertheless critical form of courage, which achieves the better outcome through a willingness to replace conflict with cooperation.

A few weeks later, Sanders happened to see the vice president. Instead of glaring reproachfully at Sanders or ignoring him, the VP shook his hand respectfully and said, "It's a pleasure working with you." The memo, which demonstrated a level of professionalism the executive himself had failed to display, paid off. Whereas countless others had crashed on the VP's reef, Sanders preserved an important relationship for his division and for himself. He also learned that he could deal with a tough customer in a creative way.

Selecting the Right Time

Desmond Tutu has described good leaders as having an uncanny sense of timing. "The real leader," he writes, knows "when to make concessions, when to compromise, when to employ the art of losing the battle in order to win the war."

It can be argued that when someone is confronted by a situation that requires courage, the question of timing should be irrelevant. We assume that in spear-in-the-sand situations, when much is at stake and emotions are running high, brave people don't hesitate to act. This may be true in emergency situations, but a single-minded rush to action in business is usually foolish.

Consider what happened when one group of senior managers pressured their CEO, who was in his seventies, to produce a succession plan a year before he was ready to do so. The CEO, who had always treated his managers like family, was deeply hurt. Though he wasn't opposed to the notion of succession planning, he considered the forcing of it premature and impertinent. Had the managers waited, the CEO later told me, they would have accomplished their mission. But they were adamant. The CEO's anger grew; he edged out one manager, and the others were soon looking for new jobs.

Although emotion is always in the mix, and may even be an asset when making a courageous move, the following questions can help in logically calculating whether the time is right:

- Why am I pursuing this now?
- Am I contemplating a considered action or an impulsive one?
- How long would it take to become better prepared? Is that too long?
- What are the pros and cons of waiting a day, two days, a week or more?
- What are the political obstacles? Can these be either removed or reduced in the near future?
- Can I take steps now that will create a foundation for a courageous move later?
- Am I emotionally and mentally prepared to take this risk?
- Do I have the expertise, communication skills, track record, and credibility to make this work?

Spending too much time on any or all of these questions, of course, can lead you into Hamlet's trap, and the opportunity for courage may pass you by. At the same time, too little consideration may result in an o'er-hasty leap. It's important to remember that courageous action in business is for the most part deliberative. Real emergencies are rare. Time may well be on your side.

Before you make your move, it's critical to marshal sufficient support, information, or evidence to improve your odds of success. The sisters Cori and Kerri Rigsby were veteran employees of E.A. Renfroe, a firm that helps State Farm and other insurance companies adjust disaster claims. Following an influx of claims by Hurricane Katrina victims, the Rigsbys found indications that State Farm was pressuring engineers to alter their conclusions about storm damage so that policyholders' claims could be denied. The sisters could have gone public with the first or second piece of evidence, but they were wise enough to know that they needed much more. They spent months collecting 15,000 pages' worth of internal reports, memos, e-mails, and claims, which they turned over to federal and state regulators. They then went to work as consultants for the Scruggs Katrina Group, which was organized to sue insurance companies on behalf of thousands of policyholders.

My research indicates that those who act courageously in business settings have an instinct for opportunity. They read situations quickly, but they are never reckless. If they sense that the emotional climate is not right for a frontal assault, or that history or politics raises insurmountable obstacles, they pause, reflect, and consider another time or route. If they feel outmatched or lack the skill or stamina to go the distance, they continue to gather their resources and wait for a more propitious moment.

Choosing the right time is the most difficult part of the courage calculation; it takes a deep sensitivity to one's surroundings and a great deal of patience.

Developing Contingency Plans

Faced with having to take a risk, most people make only one attempt: They ring the doorbell, and if a response is not forthcoming, they give up and go away. Those who accomplish their primary and secondary goals try knocking at the back door, tapping at a window, or even returning a second time.

Winning in risky situations often requires being what you haven't been, thinking as you haven't thought, and acting as you haven't acted. The better developed your contingency plans are, the likelier it is you'll achieve your primary and secondary goals. But before deciding how to proceed, it's important to account for possible failure. If you don't meet your objective, what then? Will your team lose credibility? Will you think about resigning? If not, how might you salvage your job or reputation? Can failure be converted into something positive?

Contingency planning is really about resourcefulness. People who take bold risks and succeed are versatile thinkers; they ready themselves with alternative routes. Tania Modic, for example, decided that if things went badly after her risky move, she would call the bank chairman, with whom she had a good rapport, and explain her decision. She could promise never to step out of line again. She figured that asking forgiveness after the fact was a better option than asking permission beforehand. She believed that if she got into trouble, one good word from the chairman would help her case. She even invited him to listen in on the phone call in which her superiors asked her to explain herself. As it turned out, she didn't need the chairman's support; but knowing that she could probably get it had emboldened her.

Courageous managers prepare themselves for any eventuality, including worst-case scenarios. Alison May was one of a group of stock traders attending a conflict-resolution workshop. All the attendees were young, bright, and capable, but also mutually antagonistic and unrelentingly competitive. They were courteous during the workshop, even flattering one another; but their level of conflict had reached pathological proportions, and May was disgusted by the vicious backbiting and hypocrisy of the group. She spoke up: "Who are we kidding? We despise each other most of the time." Looking directly into the eyes of her colleagues, she proceeded to describe their most flagrant transgressions. Then one red-faced trader pointed a finger at another and the venom spilled. Attacks and counterattacks flooded the air, but the group was honestly confronting its demons. Progress was made and remedies agreed to, all because May stepped up to the plate.

May had thought long and hard about the worst possible consequence: that her candor would motivate the others to get her fired. She knew that she could get another job. In fact, her most liberating contingency plan was, as she put it, to "work at McDonald's flipping burgers" rather than remain in the vipers' pit. This gave her the freedom to speak up. To her relief, the group didn't hold her outburst against her. On some level, its members were relieved to have the issues aired, and the senior VP at the workshop was impressed. May went on to become the CFO of the outdoor-clothing retailer Patagonia and, later, the CEO of the gift-catalogue company RedEnvelope.

ALISON MAY ONCE UNDERTOOK an exercise that can be useful to anyone wishing to cultivate professional courage. She wrote down the five most critical conditions for any future endeavor: that she be doing meaningful work she loved; that she be proud of the company for which she worked and proud to tell people she worked there; that at least half the company's employees and senior managers be women; that the company have a higher mission and a product that was fun, valuable, or beneficial to society; and that the company's values match her own. Throughout her career, she has measured courageous risks against this template.

In the end, courage in business rests on priorities that serve a personal, an organizational, or a societal philosophy. When this philosophy is buttressed by clear, obtainable primary and secondary goals, an evaluation of their importance, a favorable power base, a careful assessment of risks versus benefits, appropriate timing, and well-developed contingency plans, managers are better empowered to make bold moves that serve their organizations, their careers, and their own sense of personal worth.

Originally published in January 2007
Reprint R0701E; HBR OnPoint 1726

What to Ask the Person in the Mirror

ROBERT S. KAPLAN

Executive Summary

EVERY LEADER GETS OFF TRACK from time to time. But as leaders rise through the ranks, they have fewer and fewer opportunities for honest and direct feedback. Their bosses are no longer monitoring their actions, and by the time management missteps have a negative impact on business results, it's usually too late to make course corrections that will set things right. Therefore, it is wise to go through a self-assessment, to periodically step back from the bustle of running a business and ask some key questions of yourself.

Author Robert S. Kaplan, who during his 22-year career at Goldman Sachs chaired the firm's senior leadership training efforts and cochaired its partnership committee, identifies seven areas for self-reflection: vision and priorities, managing time, feedback, succession planning, evaluation and alignment, leading under pressure, and staying true to yourself. The author sets out a series of questions in each of the areas, illustrating the impact of self-assessment through vivid accounts of real executives.

Although the questions sound simple, people are often shocked–even horrified–by their own answers. Executives are aware that they should be focusing on their most important priorities, for instance, but without stepping back to reflect, few actually know where they are allocating their time. Kaplan advocates writing down what you do every working hour for a week and checking how well your actions match up with your intentions. As for feedback, managers should ask themselves whether they're getting truthful evaluations from their subordinates. (In all likelihood, they aren't.) It takes time and discipline to persuade your employees to tell you about your failings.

IF YOU'RE LIKE MOST SUCCESSFUL LEADERS, you were, in the early stages of your career, given plenty of guidance and support. You were closely monitored, coached, and mentored. But as you moved up the ladder, the sources of honest and useful feedback became fewer, and after a certain point, you were pretty much on your own. Now, your boss—if you have one—is no longer giving much consideration to your day-to-day actions. By the time any mistakes come to light, it's probably too late to fix them—or your boss's perceptions of you. And by the time your management missteps negatively affect your business results, it's usually too late to make corrections that will get you back on course.

No matter how talented and successful you are, you will make mistakes. You will develop bad habits. The world will change subtly, without your even noticing, and behaviors that once worked will be rendered ineffective. Over a 22-year career at Goldman Sachs, I had the opportunity to run various businesses and to work with or coach numerous business leaders. I chaired the firm's senior leadership training efforts and cochaired its partnership committee, which focused on reviews, promotions, and development of managing directors. Through this experience and subsequent interviews with a large number of executives in a broad range of industries, I have observed that even outstanding leaders invariably struggle through stretches of their careers where they get off track for some period of time.

It's hard to see it when you're in the midst of it; changes in the environment, competitors, or even personal circumstances can quietly guide you off your game. I have learned that a key characteristic of highly successful leaders is not that they figure out how to always stay on course, but that they develop techniques to help them recognize a deteriorating situation and get back on track as quickly as possible. In my experience, the best way to do that is to step back regularly, say every three to six months (and certainly whenever things feel as though they aren't going well), and honestly ask yourself some questions about how you're doing and what you may need to do differently. As simple as this process sounds, people are often shocked by their own answers to basic management and leadership questions.

One manager in a large financial services company who had been passed over for promotion told me he was quite surprised by his year-end performance review, which highlighted several management issues that had not been previously brought to his attention. His boss read several comments from the review that faulted him for poor communication, failure to effectively articulate a strategy for the business, and a tendency to isolate himself from his team. He believed that the review was unfair. After 15 years at the company, he began to feel confused and misunderstood and wondered whether he still had a future there. He decided to seek feedback directly from five of his key contributors and longtime collaborators. In one-on-one meetings, he asked them for blunt feedback and advice. He was shocked to hear that they were highly critical of several of his recent actions, were confused about the direction he wanted to take the business, and felt he no longer valued their input. Their feedback helped him see that he had been so immersed in the day-to-day business that he had failed to step back and think about what he was doing. This was a serious wake-up call. He immediately took steps to change his behavior and address these issues. His review the following year was dramatically better, he was finally promoted, and his business's performance improved. The manager was lucky to have received this feedback in time to get his career back on track, although he regretted that he had waited for a negative review to ask basic questions about his leadership activities. He promised himself he would not make that mistake again.

In this article, I outline seven types of questions that leaders should ask themselves on some periodic basis. I am not suggesting that there is a "right" answer to any of them or that they all will resonate with a given executive at any point in time. I am suggesting that successful executives can regularly improve their performance and preempt serious business problems by stepping back and taking the time to ask themselves certain key questions.

Vision and Priorities

It's surprising how often business leaders fail to ask themselves: *How frequently do I communicate a vision and priorities for my business? Would my employees, if asked, be able to articulate the vision and priorities?* Many leaders have, on paper, a wealth of leadership talents: interpersonal, strategic, and analytic skills; a knack for team building; and certainly the ability to develop a vision. Unfortunately, in the press of day-to-day activities, they often don't adequately communicate the vision to the organization, and in particular, they don't convey it in a way that helps their people understand what they are supposed to be doing to drive the business. It is very difficult to lead people if they don't have a firm grasp of where they're heading and what's expected of them.

This was the problem at a large *Fortune 200* company that had decided to invest in its 1,000 top managers by having them attend an intensive, two-day management-training program, 100 at a time. Before each session, the participants went through a 360-degree nonevaluative review in which critical elements of their individual performance were ranked by ten of their subordinates. The company's senior management looked at the results, focusing on the top five and bottom five traits for each group. Despite this being an extremely well-managed firm, the ability to articulate a vision ranked in the bottom five for almost every group. Managers at that company did articulate a vision, but the feedback from their subordinates strongly indicated that they were not communicating it frequently or clearly enough to meet their people's tremendous hunger for guidance.

Employees want to know where the business is going and what they need to focus on. As the world changes, they want to know how the business vision and priorities might change along with it. While managers are taught to actively communicate, many either unintentionally undercommunicate or fail to articulate specific priorities that would give meaning to their vision. However often you think you discuss vision and strategy, you may not be doing it frequently enough or in sufficient detail to suit the needs of your people. Look at the CEO of an emerging biotechnology company, who was quite frustrated with what he saw as a lack of alignment within his top management team. He strongly believed that the company needed to do a substantial equity financing within the next 18 months, but his senior managers wanted to wait a few years until two or three of the company's key drugs were further along in the FDA approval process. They preferred to tell their story to investors when the company was closer to generating revenue. When I asked him about the vision for the company, the CEO sheepishly realized that he had never actually written down a vision statement. He had a well-articulated tactical plan relating to each of the company's specific product efforts but no fully formed vision that would give further context to these efforts. He decided to organize an off-site meeting for his senior management team to discuss and specifically articulate a vision for the company.

After a vigorous debate, the group quickly agreed on a vision and strategic priorities. They realized that in order to achieve their shared goals, the business would in fact require substantial financing sooner rather than later—or they would need to scale back some of the initiatives that were central to their vision for the company. Once they fully appreciated this trade-off, they understood what the CEO was trying to accomplish and left the meeting united about their financing strategy. The CEO was quite surprised at how easy it had been to bring the members of his leadership team together. Because they agreed on where they were going as a company, specific issues were much easier to resolve.

A common pitfall in articulating a vision is a failure to boil it down to a manageable list of initiatives. Culling the list involves thinking through and then making difficult choices and trade-off decisions. These choices communicate volumes to your people about how they should be spending their time. I spoke with the manager of a national sales force who felt frustrated that his direct reports were not focusing on the tasks necessary to achieve their respective regional sales goals. As a result, sales were growing at a slower rate than budgeted at the beginning of the year. When I asked him to enumerate the three to five key priorities he expected his salespeople to focus on, he paused and then explained that there were 15 and it would be very difficult to narrow the list down to five.

Even as he spoke, a light went on in his head. He realized why there might be a disconnect between him and his people: They didn't know precisely what he wanted because he had not told them in a prioritized, and therefore actionable, manner. He reflected on this issue for the next two weeks, thinking at length about his own experience as a regional manager and consulting with various colleagues. He then picked three priorities that he felt were crucial to achieving sales growth. The most important of these involved a major new-business targeting exercise followed by a substantial new-prospect calling effort. The regional managers immediately understood and began focusing on these initiatives. The fact is that having 15 priorities is the same as having none at all. Managers have a responsibility to translate their vision into a manageable number of priorities that their subordinates can understand and act on.

Failing to communicate your vision and priorities has direct costs to you in terms of time and business effectiveness. It's hard to delegate if your people don't have a good sense of the big picture; hence you end up doing more work yourself. This issue can cascade through the organization if your direct reports are, in turn, unable to communicate a vision and effectively leverage their own subordinates.

Managing Time

The second area to question is painfully simple and closely relates to the first: *How am I spending my time?* Once you know your priorities, you need to determine whether you're spending your time—your most precious asset—in a way that will allow you to achieve them. For example, if your two major priorities are senior talent development and global expansion but you're spending the majority of your time on domestic operational and administrative matters that could be delegated, then you need to recognize there is a disconnect and you'd better make some changes.

It's such a simple question, yet many leaders, myself included, just can't accurately answer at times. When leaders finally do track their time, they're often surprised by what they find. Most of us go through periods where unexpected events and day-to-day chaos cause us to be reactive rather than acting on a proscribed plan. Crises, surprises, personnel issues, and interruptions make the workweek seem like a blur. I have recommended to many leaders that they track how they spend each hour of each day for one week, then categorize the hours into types of activities: business development, people management, and strategic planning, for example. For most executives, the results of this exercise are startling—even horrifying—with obvious disconnects between what their top priorities are and how they are spending their time.

For example, the CEO of a midsize manufacturing company was frustrated because he was working 70 hours a week and never seemed to catch up. His family life suffered, and, at work, he was constantly unavailable for his people and major customers. I suggested he step back and review how he was managing his time hour-by-hour over the course of a week. We sat down to examine the results and noticed that he was spending a substantial amount of time approving company expenditures, some for as little as $500—this in a business with $500 million in sales. Sitting in my office, he struggled to explain why he had not delegated some portion of this responsibility; it turned out that the activity was a holdover from a time when the company was much smaller. By delegating authority to approve recurring operating expenses below $25,000, he realized he could save as much as 15 hours per week. He was amazed that he had not recognized this issue and made this simple change much earlier.

How you spend your time is an important question not only for you but for your team. People tend to take their cues from the leader when it comes to time management—therefore, you want to make sure there's a match between your actions, your business priorities, and your team's activities. The CEO of a rapidly growing, 300-person professional services firm felt that, to build the business, senior managers needed to develop stronger and more substantive relationships with clients. This meant that senior professionals would need to spend significantly more time out of their offices in meetings with clients. When asked how his own time was being spent, the CEO was unable to answer. After tracking it for a week, he was shocked to find that he was devoting a tremendous amount of his time to administrative activities related to managing the firm.

He realized that the amount of attention he was paying to these matters did not reflect the business's priorities and was sending a confusing message to his people. He immediately began pushing himself to delegate a number of these administrative tasks and increase the amount of time he spent on the road with customers, setting a powerful example for his people. He directed each of his senior managers to do a similar time-allocation exercise to ensure they were dedicating sufficient time to clients.

Of course, the way a leader spends his or her time must be tailored to the needs of the business, which may vary depending on time of year, personnel changes, and external factors. The key here is, whatever you decide, time allocation needs to be a conscious decision that fits your vision and priorities for the business. Given the pressure of running a business, it is easy to lose focus, so it's important to ask yourself this question periodically. Just as you would step back and review a major investment decision, you need to dispassionately review the manner in which you invest your time.

Feedback

When you think about the ways you approach feedback, you should first ask: *Do I give people timely, direct, and constructive feedback?* And second: *Do I have five or six junior people who will tell me things I don't want to hear but need to hear?*

If they're like most ambitious employees, your subordinates want to be coached and developed in a truthful and direct manner. They want to get feedback while there's still an opportunity to act on it; if you've waited until the year-end review, it's often too late. In my experience, well-intentioned managers typically fail to give blunt, direct, and timely feedback to their subordinates.

One reason for this failure is that managers are often afraid that constructive feedback and criticism will demoralize their employees. In addition, critiquing a professional in a frank and timely manner may be perceived as overly confrontational. Lastly, many managers fear that this type of feedback will cause employees not to like them. Consequently, leaders often wait until year-end performance reviews. The year-end review is evaluative (that is, the verdict on the year) and therefore is not conducive to constructive coaching. The subordinate is typically on the defensive and not as open to criticism. This approach creates surprises, often unpleasant ones, which undermine trust and dramatically reduce the confidence of the subordinate in the manager.

The reality is that managers who don't give immediate and direct feedback often are "liked" until year-end—at which time they wind up being strongly disliked. If employees have fallen short of expectations, the failing is reflected in bonuses, raises, and promotions. The feeling of injustice can be enormous. What's worse is the knowledge that if an employee had received feedback earlier in the year, it is likely that he or she would have made meaningful efforts to improve and address the issues.

While people do like to hear positive feedback, ultimately, they desperately want to know the truth, and I have rarely seen someone quit over hearing the truth or being challenged to do better—unless it's too late. On the contrary, I would argue that people are more likely to stay if they understand what issues they need to address and they trust you to bring those issues to their attention in a straightforward and prompt fashion. They gain confidence that you will work with them to develop their skills and that they won't be blindsided at the end of the year. Employees who don't land a hoped-for promotion will be much more likely to forgive you if you've told them all along what they need to do better, even if they haven't gotten there yet. They may well redouble their efforts to prove to you that they can overcome these issues.

During my career at Goldman Sachs, I consistently found that professional development was far more effective when coaching and direct feedback were given to employees throughout the year—well in advance of the annual performance review process. Internal surveys of managing directors showed that, in cases where feedback was confined to the year-end review, satisfaction with career development was dramatically lower than when it was offered throughout the year.

As hard as it is to give effective and timely feedback, many leaders find it much more challenging to get feedback from their employees. Once you reach a certain stage of your career, junior people are in a much better position than your boss to tell you how you're doing. They see you in your day-to-day activities, and they experience your decisions directly. Your boss, at this stage, is much more removed and, as a result, typically needs to talk to your subordinates to assess your performance at the end of the year. In order to avoid your own year-end surprises, you need to develop a network of junior professionals who are willing to give you constructive feedback. The problem is that, while your direct reports know what you are doing wrong, most of them are not dying to tell you. With good reason—there's very little upside and a tremendous amount of downside. The more senior and the more important you become, the less your subordinates will tell you the "awful truth"—things that are difficult to hear but that you need to know.

It takes a concerted effort to cultivate subordinates who will advise and coach you. It also takes patience and some relentlessness. When I ask subordinates for constructive feedback, they will typically and predictably tell me that I'm doing "very well." When I follow up and ask "What should I do differently?" they respond, "Nothing that I can think of." If I challenge them by saying, "There must be something!" still they say, "Nothing comes to mind." I then ask them to sit back and think—we have plenty of time. By this time, beads of sweat begin to become visible on their foreheads. After an awkward silence, they will eventually come up with something—and it's often devastating to hear. It's devastating because it's a damning criticism and because you know it's true.

What you do with this feedback is critical. If you act on it, you will improve your performance. Equally important, you will take a big step in building trust and laying the groundwork for a channel of honest feedback. When subordinates see that you respond positively to suggestions, they will often feel more ownership in the business and in your success. They'll learn to give you criticisms on their own initiative because they know you will actually appreciate it and do something with it. Developing a network of "coaching" subordinates will help you take action to identify your own leadership issues and meaningfully improve your performance.

Succession Planning

Another question that managers know is important yet struggle to answer affirmatively is: *Have I, at least in my own mind, picked one or more potential successors?* This issue is critical because if you aren't identifying potential successors, you are probably not delegating as extensively as you should and you may well be a decision-making bottleneck. Being a bottleneck invariably means that you are not spending enough time on vital leadership priorities and are failing to develop your key subordinates. Ironically, when leaders believe they are so talented that they can perform tasks far better than any of their subordinates and therefore insist on doing the tasks themselves, they will typically cause their businesses to underperform, and, ultimately, their careers will suffer as well.

The succession question also has significant implications that cascade through an organization: If leaders do not develop successors, then the organization may lack a sufficient number of leaders to successfully grow the business. Worse, if junior employees are not developed, they may leave the firm for better opportunities elsewhere. For these reasons, many well-managed companies will hesitate to promote executives who have failed to develop successors.

It is sufficient to identify possible successors without actually telling them you've done so—as long as this identification causes you to manage them differently. In particular, you will want to delegate more of your major responsibilities to these professionals. This will speed their maturation and prepare them to step up to the next level. By giving demanding assignments to these subordinates, you strongly signal an interest in their development and career progression—which will encourage them to turn down offers from competitors. Leaders who do this are much better able to keep their teams together and avoid losing up-and-coming stars to competitors.

A loss of talent is highly damaging to a company. It is particularly painful if you could have retained key employees by simply challenging them more intensively. I spoke with a division head of a large company who was concerned about what he perceived to be a talent deficit in his organization. He felt that he could not use his time to the fullest because he viewed his direct reports as incapable of assuming some of his major responsibilities. He believed this talent deficit was keeping him from launching several new product and market initiatives. In the midst of all this, he lost two essential subordinates over six months—each had left to take on increased responsibilities at major competitors. He had tried to persuade them to stay, emphasizing that he was actively considering them for significant new leadership assignments. Because they had not seen evidence of this previously, they were skeptical and left anyway. I asked him whether, prior to the defections, he had identified them (or anyone else) as potential successors, put increased responsibilities in their hands, or actively ratcheted up his coaching of these professionals. He answered that, in the chaos of daily events and in the effort to keep up with the business, he had not done so. He also admitted that he had underestimated the potential of these two employees and realized he was probably underestimating the abilities of several others in the company. He immediately sat down and made a list of potential stars and next to each name wrote out a career and responsibility game plan. He immediately got to work on this formative succession plan, although he suspected that he had probably waited too long already.

When you're challenging and testing people, you delegate to them more often, which frees you to focus on the most critical strategic matters facing the business. This will make you more successful and a more attractive candidate for your own future promotion.

Evaluation and Alignment

The world is constantly changing. Your customers' needs change; your business evolves (going, for instance, from high growth to mature); new products and distribution methods emerge as threats. When these changes happen, if you don't change along with them, you can get seriously out of alignment. The types of people you hire, the way you organize them, the economic incentives you offer them, and even the nature of the tasks you delegate no longer create the culture and outcomes that are critical to the success of your business. It's your job to make sure that the design of your organization is aligned with the key success factors for the business. Ask yourself: *Am I attuned to changes in the business environment that would require a change in the way we organize and run our business?*

Such clear-sightedness is, of course, hard to achieve. As a leader, you may be too close to the business to see subtle changes that are continually occurring. Because you probably played a central role in building and designing the business, it may be emotionally very difficult to make meaningful changes. You may have to fire certain employees—people you recruited and hired. You may also have to acknowledge that you made some mistakes and be open to changing your own operating style in a way that is uncomfortable for some period of time.

Because of the difficulty in facing these issues, it's sometimes wise to call on high-potential subordinates to take a fresh look at the business. This approach can be quite effective because junior employees are often not as emotionally invested as you are and can see more objectively what needs to be done. This approach is also a good way to challenge your future leaders and give them a valuable development experience. You'll give them a chance to exercise their strategic skills; you'll get a glimpse of their potential (which relates to the earlier discussion of succession planning), and you might just get some terrific new ideas for how to run the business.

This approach worked for the CEO of a high technology business in northern California, whose company had been one of the early innovators in its product space but, in recent years, had begun to falter and lose market share. In its early days, the company's primary success factors had been product innovation and satisfying customer needs. It had aggressively hired innovative engineers and marketing personnel. As new competitors emerged, customers began to focus more on cost and service (in the form of more sophisticated applications development). Stepping back, the CEO sensed that he needed to redesign the company with a different mix of people, a new organization, and a revised incentive structure. Rather than try to come up with a new model himself, he asked a more junior group of executives to formulate a new company design as if they had a "clean sheet of paper." Their study took a number of weeks, but upon completion, it led to several recommendations that the CEO immediately began to implement. For example, they suggested colocating the engineering and sales departments and creating integrated account coverage teams. They also recommended that the company push more of its engineers to interact with customers and focus on this skill in recruiting. The CEO regretted that he had not asked the question—and conducted this assignment—12 months earlier.

Even the most successful business is susceptible to new challenges posed by a changing world. Effective executives regularly look at their businesses with a clean sheet of paper—seeking advice and other perspectives from people who are less emotionally invested in the business—in order to determine whether key aspects of the way they run their organizations are still appropriate.

Leading Under Pressure

Pressure is a part of business. Changes in business conditions create urgent problems. New entrants in the market demand a competitive response. Valued employees quit, often at the most inopportune times. Leaders and their teams, no matter how smart they are, make mistakes.

The interesting thing about stressful events is that they affect each person differently—what causes you anxiety may not bother someone else, and vice versa. For some, extreme anxiety may be triggered by the prospect of a promotion; for others, by making a serious mistake; still others, by losing a piece of business to a competitor. Regardless of the source of stress, every leader experiences it, so a good question to ask yourself is: *How do I behave under pressure, and what signals am I sending my employees?*

As a leader, you're watched closely. During a crisis, your people watch you with a microscope, noting every move you make. In such times, your subordinates learn a great deal about you and what you really believe, as opposed to what you say. Do you accept responsibility for mistakes, or do you look for someone to blame? Do you support your employees, or do you turn on them? Are you cool and calm, or do you lose your temper? Do you stand up for what you believe, or do you take the expedient route and advocate what you think your seniors want to hear? You need to be self-aware enough to recognize the situations that create severe anxiety for you and manage your behavior to avoid sending unproductive messages to your people.

I've met a number of leaders who behave in a very composed and thoughtful manner the great majority of the time. Unfortunately, when they're under severe stress, they react in ways that set a very negative tone. They inadvertently train their employees to mimic that behavior and behave in a similar fashion. If your instinct is to shield yourself from blame, to take credit rather than sharing it with your subordinates, or to avoid admitting when you have made a mistake, you will give your employees license to do the same.

The CEO of a large asset-management firm was frustrated that he was unable to build a culture of accountability and teamwork in his growing business. At his request, I spoke to a number of his team members. I asked in particular about the actions of the CEO when investments they recommended declined in value. They recounted his frequent temper tantrums and accusatory diatribes, which led to an overwhelming atmosphere of blame and finger-pointing. The investment decisions had, in fact, been made jointly through a carefully constructed process involving portfolio managers, industry analysts, and the CEO. As a result of these episodes, employees learned that when investments went wrong it would be good to try to find someone else to blame. Hearing these stories, the CEO realized his actions under pressure were far more persuasive to employees than his speeches about teamwork and culture. He understood that he would have to learn to moderate his behavior under stress and, subsequently, took steps to avoid reacting so angrily to negative investment results. He also became more aware that subordinates typically felt quite regretful and demoralized when their investments declined and were more likely to need a pat on the back and coaching than a kick in the pants.

It's extremely difficult to expect employees to alert you to looming problems when they fear your reaction—and even more so when they think it's better to distance themselves from potential problems. This can create an atmosphere where surprises are, in fact, more likely as the company's natural early-warning system has been inadvertently disarmed. If you have created this kind of culture, it is quite unlikely that you will learn about problems from subordinates spontaneously—unless they want to commit career suicide.

Part of the process of maturing as a leader is learning to step back and think about what creates pressure for you, being self-aware in these situations, and disciplining your behavior to ensure that you act in a manner consistent with your core values.

Staying True to Yourself

Most business leaders ask themselves whether their leadership style fits the needs of their business. Fewer managers ask whether their style also fits their own beliefs and personality. The question here is: *Does my leadership style reflect who I truly am?*

A business career is a marathon, not a sprint, and if you aren't true to yourself, eventually you're going to wear down. As you are developing in your career, it is advisable to observe various leadership styles, and pick and choose elements that feel comfortable to you. Bear in mind, though, that observing and adopting aspects of other styles does not mean you should try to be someone else. During my career, I was fortunate to have had several superb bosses and colleagues with distinctive and unique leadership skills. While I tried to adopt some of their techniques, I also learned that I needed to develop an overall style that fit my unique skills and personality. Your style needs to fit you; even an unorthodox style can be enormously effective if it reflects your skills, values, and personality.

As you become more senior, you'll need to ask yourself an additional set of questions relating to style: *Do I assert myself sufficiently, or have I become tentative? Am I too politically correct? Does worry about my next promotion or my year-end bonus cause me to pull punches or hesitate to clearly express my views?* In many companies, ambitious executives may try to avoid confronting sensitive issues or making waves. Worse than that, they may spend an inordinate amount of energy trying to ascertain what their boss thinks and then act like they think the same thing. If they're very skilled at this, they may even get a chance to make their comments before the boss has a chance to express his opinion—and feel the warm glow of approval from the boss.

The problem is that confrontation and disagreement are crucial to effective decision making. Some of the worst decisions I've been involved in were made after a group of intelligent people had unanimously agreed to the course of action—though, later, several participants admitted that they had misgivings but were hesitant to diverge from the apparent group consensus. Conversely, it's hard for me to recall a poor decision I was involved in that was made after a thorough debate in which opposing views were vigorously expressed (even if I disagreed with the ultimate decision). Companies need their leaders to express strongly held views rather than mimic what they believe to be the party line. As a leader, therefore, you must ask yourself whether you are expressing your views or holding back and being too politic. At the same time, leaders must encourage their own subordinates to express their unvarnished opinions, make waves as appropriate, and stop tiptoeing around significant issues.

SUCCESSFUL LEADERS periodically struggle during stretches of their careers. To get back on track, they must devise techniques for stepping back, getting perspective, and developing a new game plan. In this process, having the answers is often far less important than taking time to ask yourself the right questions and gain key insights. The questions posed in this article are intended to spark your thinking. Only a subset of these may resonate with you, and you may find it more useful to come up with your own list. In either event, a self-questioning process conducted on a periodic basis will help you work through leadership challenges and issues that you invariably must tackle over the course of your career.

Testing Yourself

To assess your performance and stay on track, you should step back and ask yourself certain key questions.

Vision and Priorities

In the press of day-to-day activities, leaders often fail to adequately communicate their vision to the organization, and in particular, they don't communicate it in a way that helps their subordinates determine where to focus their own efforts.

How often do I communicate a vision for my business?

Have I identified and communicated three to five key priorities to achieve that vision?

If asked, would my employees be able to articulate the vision and priorities?

Managing Time

Leaders need to know how they're spending their time. They also need to ensure that their time allocation (and that of their subordinates) matches their key priorities.

How am I spending my time? Does it match my key priorities?

How are my subordinates spending their time? Does that match the key priorities for the business?

Feedback

Leaders often fail to coach employees in a direct and timely fashion and, instead, wait until the year-end review. This approach may lead to unpleasant surprises and can undermine effective professional development. Just as important, leaders need to cultivate subordinates who can give them advice and feedback during the year.

Do I give people timely and direct feedback that they can act on?

Do I have five or six junior subordinates who will tell me things I may not want to hear but need to hear?

Succession Planning

When leaders fail to actively plan for succession, they do not delegate sufficiently and may become decision-making bottlenecks. Key employees may leave if they are not actively groomed and challenged.

Have I, at least in my own mind, picked one or more potential successors?

Am I coaching them and giving them challenging assignments?

Am I delegating sufficiently? Have I become a decision-making bottleneck?

Evaluation and Alignment

The world is constantly changing, and leaders need to be able to adapt their businesses accordingly.

Is the design of my company still aligned with the key success factors for the business?

If I had to design my business with a clean sheet of paper, how would I design it? How would it differ from the current design?

Should I create a task force of subordinates to answer these questions and make recommendations to me?

Leading Under Pressure

A leader's actions in times of stress are watched closely by subordinates and have a profound impact on the culture of the firm and employees' behavior. Successful leaders need to be aware of their own stress triggers and consciously modulate their behavior during these periods to make sure they are acting in ways that are consistent with their beliefs and core values.

What types of events create pressure for me? How do I behave under pressure?

What signals am I sending my subordinates? Are these signals helpful, or are they undermining the success of my business?

Staying True to Yourself

Successful executives develop leadership styles that fit the needs of their business but also fit their own beliefs and personality.

Is my leadership style comfortable? Does it reflect who I truly am?

Do I assert myself sufficiently, or have I become tentative?

Am I too politically correct?

Does worry about my next promotion or bonus cause me to pull punches or hesitate to express my views?

Originally published in January 2007
Reprint R0701H; HBR OnPoint 1730

The CEO's Second Act

DAVID A. NADLER

Executive Summary

WHEN A CEO LEAVES because of performance problems, the company typically recruits someone thought to be better equipped to fix what the departing executive couldn't–or wouldn't. The board places its confidence in the new person because of the present dilemma's similarity to some previous challenge that he or she dealt with successfully. But familiar problems are inevitably succeeded by less familiar ones, for which the specially selected CEO is not quite so qualified. More often than not, the experiences, skills, and temperament that yielded triumph in Act I turn out to be unequal to Act II's difficulties. In fact, the approaches that worked so brilliantly in Act I may be the very opposite of what is needed in Act II.

The CEO has four choices: refuse to change, in which case he or she will be replaced; realize that the next act requires new skills and learn them; downsize or circumscribe his or her role to compensate for deficiencies; or line up a successor who is qualified to fill a role to which the incumbent's skills and interests are no longer suited. Hewlett-Packard's Carly Fiorina exemplifies the first alternative; Merrill Lynch's Stanley O'Neal the second; Google's Sergey Brin and Larry Page the third; and Quest Diagnostics' Ken Freeman the fourth. All but the first option are reasonable responses to the challenges presented in the second acts of most CEOs' tenures. And all but the first require a power of observation, a propensity for introspection, and a strain of humility that are rare in the ranks of the very people who need those qualities most.

There are four essential steps executives can take to discern that they have entered new territory and to respond accordingly: *recognition* that their leadership style and approach are no longer working; *acceptance* of others' advice on why performance is faltering; *analysis and understanding* of the nature of the Act II shift; and, finally, *decision and action.*

THE C-SUITE has become the hot seat. With CEOs under enormous pressure to deliver the outstanding performance investors demand—and to satisfy other, often conflicting constituencies—it is no wonder that the pace of CEO turnover is accelerating. The latest Booz Allen Hamilton CEO succession study found that 15.3% of CEOs worldwide and 16.2% in North America left office in 2005. That's an increase since 1995 of 70% globally and 54% in North America. What's more, a third of the departures in the most recent survey were "nonroutine"—that is, they occurred before the scheduled succession date, usually because of performance problems.

Typically, the early departure of a CEO leads to the recruitment of someone thought to be better equipped to fix what the last CEO couldn't, or wouldn't. The new leader arrives with a mandate to change course or, in the most extreme circumstances, to save a sinking ship. The board places its confidence in him because of the present dilemma's similarity to some previous challenge he dealt with successfully, such as reshuffling a portfolio, slashing costs, increasing market share, or negotiating with regulators.

Facing a familiar problem, the CEO can be expected to do what he was hired to do. Indeed, research presented in "Are Leaders Portable?" by Boris Groysberg, Andrew N. McLean, and Nitin Nohria (HBR May 2006), indicates that leaders succeed when the skills demanded in their new positions directly draw upon the executives' professional backgrounds and experiences. But familiar problems are inevitably succeeded by less familiar ones, for which the specially selected CEO is not quite so qualified. More often than not, the experiences, skills, and temperament that yielded triumph in Act I turn out to be unequal to Act II's difficulties. In fact, the approaches that worked so brilliantly in Act I may be the very opposite of what is needed to bring Act II to a happy resolution.

As the drama unfolds, the CEO has four choices: He can refuse to change, in which case he will be replaced; he can realize that the next act requires new skills and learn them; he can downsize or circumscribe his role to compensate for his deficiencies; or he can line up a successor who is qualified to fill a role to which the incumbent's skills and interests are no longer suited. Hewlett-Packard's Carly Fiorina exemplifies the first alternative; Merrill Lynch's Stanley O'Neal the second; Google's Sergey Brin and Larry Page the third; and Quest Diagnostics' Ken Freeman the fourth. All but the first option are reasonable responses to the challenges presented in the second acts of most CEOs' tenures. And all but the first require a power of observation, a propensity for introspection, and a strain of humility that are, in truth, quite rare in the ranks of the very people who need those qualities most.

Act II's Four Variations

Remake your company into one that has no place for you. Carly Fiorina is a perfect example of a CEO brought in to address a specific set of problems because of her success in dealing with similar ones elsewhere. Hewlett-Packard's board began searching for a new CEO because the company had become stodgy, inbred, bureaucratic, uncompetitive, and demoralized. HP's last groundbreaking innovation, the ink-jet printer, had been introduced 15 years earlier, in 1984, and quarterly growth was almost nonexistent. Competitors threatened to encroach on every segment of HP's business—Dell in PCs, Lexmark in printers, Sun Microsystems in servers, and IBM in solutions. So the board sought a dynamic, first-class communicator who could revive morale, restart the innovation engine, cut through the bureaucracy, and justify the reputation on which HP had been undeservedly resting for too long.

Fiorina filled the bill. Having been president of Lucent's Global Service Provider Business, she had done these things before. She set out to market her vision for HP by making speeches and appearances at high-profile events such as the World Economic Forum, courting media attention, meeting with endless groups of HP managers, and, perhaps most dramatically, becoming the public face of the company by appearing in its commercials and other advertising. Contributing to her personal mystique and sharpening HP's image was her distinction as the first woman to lead such a large, well-known company.

As outsized as her image were the steps she took to recast the organization. She laid off thousands of people and consolidated well over a hundred product groups into about a dozen to reduce redundancies and speed decision making. But only a major acquisition, she concluded, could disrupt entrenched routines and catapult HP into a commanding lead in the personal computer industry. To accomplish this, she was forced to override a boardroom minority that objected to a merger with Compaq, and she ignored those who pointed out that mergers of large companies in the high-tech arena had never worked out.

Today, even her detractors admit that the Compaq acquisition made sense. Despite boardroom tensions that exploded into a spying scandal, HP is now enjoying a growing lead over its competitors, including what was supposed to be an unstoppable Dell. But integrating two organizations and boosting operating performance in the core businesses require very different skills from developing a vision, embodying it, communicating it, and driving it through—Fiorina's proven strengths. Her continued public exposure, even after the battle was won, led to accusations that she was an incorrigible publicity hound. In the end, her reluctance to delegate led to conflict with the board, which lost confidence in her.

Remake your company—then yourself. In 2003, Stan O'Neal was engaged in deep reflection. He was finishing his first year as the CEO of Merrill Lynch, and, despite his tremendous success, he sensed it was time for a change.

Two years earlier, in July 2001, he had been named president of the company. Six weeks later, he was managing in command-and-control mode, regrouping the firm after the terrorist attacks of September 11, which killed three employees and forced the company to evacuate its heavily damaged headquarters. Additionally, Merrill Lynch was still feeling the effects of the bursting of the tech bubble a year earlier (and it would soon be hit with a wave of negative headlines about the Wall Street research scandal). The challenges required immediate action; O'Neal made painful and unpopular decisions that would be criticized by some within Merrill Lynch and second-guessed from the sidelines.

Between 2001 and 2003, O'Neal worked hard to resize and reshape the firm, cutting costs to cope with lower revenue, reengineering parts of the business to diversify revenue streams and neutralize the roller-coaster highs and lows of debt and equity trading, and reining in expansion plans that had failed to deliver.

O'Neal often found himself in a lonely position: He knew he had to rethink the firm's entire business model and challenge the "Mother Merrill" culture that had become more maternalistic than performance based. At the same time, he had to improve the morale of a shaken workforce and retain the attributes of the iconic franchise he had inherited.

By the summer of 2003, O'Neal's efforts had paid off, with Merrill Lynch posting the best first-half results in its nearly century-long history. With the firm on solid ground, he began to think longer term about what he would need to do to ensure that Merrill's future leaders would not have to face similar problems. He realized that new challenges would require Merrill's executives, himself included, to provide a substantially new kind of leadership. In other words, he understood the need to make a major shift in leadership skills in Act II, even though Act I had been a great success.

Working with an outside consultant and his senior management team, he led a process of feedback and coaching. Together they created the Merrill Lynch Leadership Model to clarify what they expected of themselves and other leaders at the firm. The model focuses on four areas critical to effective leadership: strategic thinking, business results, people leadership, and personal effectiveness.

The top 11 leaders (including O'Neal), followed by the next 200, then the next 1,000, received feedback and coaching. Changes were made in performance evaluation, rewards, talent reviews, and other mechanisms to support the new model of leadership. By 2006, objective measures revealed that Merrill's culture, which had been homogeneous, lenient, and clubby, had shifted significantly, becoming merit based, rigorous, and diverse.

Respect your limitations while growing your company. Larry Page and Sergey Brin founded Google when they were PhD candidates at Stanford. The uniquely effective Internet search engine they invented enabled their company to be one of the few healthy survivors of the dot-com crash. As their background might suggest, the founders' strong suit is writing computer code. But their ambitions for Google go well beyond spurring technical refinements of its core technology. Google now offers satellite mapping, digitalized libraries, and its own e-mail service, and its search capabilities extend to e-mail databases and company intranets. Although Page and Brin were committed to staying with the company they created, they knew they weren't professional managers or marketers or masters of strategy. So in 2001 they brought in a "grown-up," Eric Schmidt, to operate the company.

Schmidt had been the chairman and CEO of Novell for four years, and before that he was the chief technology officer at Sun Microsystems, where he led the development of Java. He is a skilled big-company executive, a seasoned marketer, and a renowned technology expert in his own right. With Schmidt as CEO, Page as president for products, and Brin as president for technology, the company has flourished beyond almost anyone's expectations. Indeed, Google provides one of the few examples of technology-oriented founders making a smooth handoff to a professional manager.

Remake your company, then move on. In 1995, Ken Freeman was named chairman and CEO of Corning Clinical Labs, the ailing medical testing business soon to be spun off from Corning. Freeman had been a Corning "lifer," having risen through the financial side to become controller while still in his early forties. He then moved through a variety of roles, among them running the company's television-glass business and serving as CFO.

Freeman found a business in shambles. Receivables sat on the books interminably; cash flow was plummeting at an alarming pace. Questionable lab results and billing practices had made the company (along with others in the industry) a target of government investigations. Freeman's drastic mandate was not to rescue the business but to get it ready to be sold. However, the troubles were so pronounced that no credible buyer stepped forward, and Corning was forced to adopt a Plan B: a spin-off of the clinical labs as an independent public company with Freeman as its chairman and CEO.

Freeman made clear to his management team that billing practices that were common in the testing industry threatened the business's survival. He quickly installed a rigorous quality process, assembled a new board, and generally pulled the company together. Having created stability, he embarked on an expansion program that culminated in the acquisition of the lab's largest competitor, SmithKline Beecham Clinical Laboratories. When the dust settled, the now renamed Quest Diagnostics was the industry leader in size, geographic reach, market share, and quality. Its stock price soared. Then, in 1999, with Quest still gathering momentum, Freeman went out to find a successor and worked with the board to put in place an orderly succession process. In 2003, at the still youthful age of 53, Freeman passed the baton to Surya Mohapatra and left the company he had built.

Why, unlike Fiorina, did Freeman leave before he had to, when in fact the board, investors, and employees wanted him to stay? Reflecting on his decision later, Freeman observed that the company's future growth would have to be organic (for one thing, Freeman had exhausted the supply of major acquisition targets). A deep understanding of medical technology, which Mohapatra possessed and Freeman lacked, was going to be a more crucial qualification for leading Quest than a flair for turnaround situations or a gift for deal making, Freeman realized.

But if so, why didn't Freeman, like O'Neal, decide to turn himself into the kind of executive Quest required? The difference was that Freeman felt most alive in the high-pressure situations of crisis and M&A. Gently moving the tiller from side to side after he had prevented the vessel from capsizing was Freeman's idea of boredom. Being not only an effective executive but a wise one, he didn't invent or precipitate crises or make ill-considered acquisitions simply to keep himself engaged. Instead he went looking for a new arena where he could find excitement and success. Today he is with KKR, engineering turnarounds at companies such as Masonite International.

The Obstacles to Coping

CEOs often face enormous challenges in their first months on the job. In her Act I, Fiorina had to symbolize leadership, as well as lead effectively, in order to achieve the transformation she sought. In his, O'Neal had to be almost inhumanly tough to shatter the culture that was impeding Merrill's progress. In theirs, Brin and Page had to devise the algorithms that would produce the most germane search results on the Internet. And in his, Freeman had to envision a company that in no way resembled the existing one.

Each of these executives performed brilliantly, as do many other CEOs who are brought in to fix specific problems. But as predictably as in a play of Shakespeare's, a successful CEO's Act I will end, and a second act will begin, sometimes imperceptibly. It usually happens before the first two years are up. (Of course, there are plenty of chief executives who are unsuited to solving the problems they were hired to overcome and who fail within the first year and a half; see the article "When CEOs Step Up to Fail," by Jay A. Conger and David A. Nadler, in the Spring 2004 issue of *Sloan Management Review.*) A career-testing ordeal arose after two years in O'Neal's case, three years in Page and Brin's, and five years in Fiorina's.

Why do so many high performers—not just those mentioned here but hundreds of others too—meet their end when Act II begins? There are several reasons. First, some CEOs are simply oblivious to the shift in its early stages. The extraordinary commitment they must make to solving the first set of problems, and their tendency to attack those aspects most likely to yield to their proven methods, somehow blind them to less familiar realities, as well as to the new leadership approaches that are required. Second, some CEOs sense the shift but fail to understand how much damage they can cause by sticking to their original approaches. CEOs are notoriously poor observers of their own behavior, and they rarely notice its unintended consequences or invite feedback. Third, some recognize the new circumstances and thus the need for a change in their modes of leadership but are incapable of transforming themselves enough to make a difference. Finally, some don't change in Act II because they don't want to. Freeman may have been capable of leading differently in Quest's next phase—he certainly understood the need to do so—but making that transformation had little appeal for him.

Leadership style is a function of years of development and experiences, and it is an outgrowth of personality and character. Achieving a dramatic change in leadership style is difficult for anyone, but it's particularly hard for people in their fifth or sixth decade who have been responsible for a long string of successes. Personality and character aside, such people have developed systems for leading, so to speak, that they can't bring themselves to jettison. In fact, when faced with resistance during Act II to their customary modes of acting, some leaders hang on more tightly than ever to the devices that have long kept them afloat.

Another way of looking at this phenomenon is that these leaders' well-worn management techniques have become inseparable from their prevailing view of themselves. In a series of landmark studies, organizational psychologist Joseph L. Moses observed the different ways in which managers deal with emerging and unfamiliar challenges. "Stylized" leaders, as he called them, cling to old and discredited approaches that have become part of their identities as executives. These leaders believe that if they were to feel their way by trial and error to a new set of responses, they would sacrifice the skills and personal qualities that gave them their successes and reputations. "Adaptive" leaders, by contrast, spend time understanding the situations confronting them and contrive strategies and approaches that fit the circumstances. Stylized managers can be extremely effective until they encounter a situation that is too dissimilar to its predecessors to yield to the proven approach. Not surprisingly, Moses found adaptive managers to be more effective overall in a range of different situations.

Psychology and learned behavior, reinforced by experience, are only half the story, however. The limitations in executives' cognitive abilities also have a role to play in CEOs' Act II reversals. A longitudinal study published by Andrew D. Henderson, Danny Miller, and Donald C. Hambrick in May 2006 compared the tenures of 98 CEOs in branded foods, an industry that the researchers describe as comparatively stable, with 228 CEOs in computers. The food companies' performance tended to improve over the course of the CEO's tenure; in computers, performance tended to peak early and diminish steadily thereafter. The authors' hypothesis is that every CEO comes to the job with a "relatively fixed" approach—a view of the world and a matching set of skills. The more dynamic the business environment, the faster those worldviews and abilities become mismatched to present realities, both competitive and organizational, and "it will be the rare executive who can greatly transform his or her mind-set, aptitudes, and skills."

As the researchers suggest, a senior executive who has built her career on being the most effective mass producer of the lowest-cost products would find it extremely difficult to adopt a strategy based on providing luxury offerings. She would be hampered by her mental habits, her values, her understanding of and interest in particular kinds of customers, and her entrenched notions of what works. Executives in the publishing industry are experiencing those pains right now. Despite their grand visions of migrating content from print to digital platforms, the majority of longtime print executives are finding it difficult to make the wrenching decisions required to facilitate the transition.

Companies that successfully identify and develop talent recognize that stylized and otherwise limited managers can be effective if matched to the right situations. They also recognize that people often need to be moved laterally when situations change or when it becomes clear that an executive has been put in the wrong position. But there is no lateral position in the company to which a CEO can be moved. When a chief executive is inflexible or unable to see a change in circumstances, the board must take actions that are inherently unpleasant and disruptive.

Four Steps to Renewal

Despite the personal and professional limitations that affect executives' ability to adapt, there are steps executives can take to discern that they have entered new territory and to respond accordingly. Here are the four essential ones.

RECOGNITION

Evidence that your leadership style and approach are no longer working can take several forms. You may notice that people aren't responding as they once did to your speeches, especially those in which you lay out your vision for the next two or three or five years, and that your initiatives are faltering. You may also find yourself clashing with your team or with your board. You may start to feel fatigued and emotionally disengaged from your work, which has started to seem like a job rather than a calling. While none of the above by itself would be proof positive that the ground has shifted, an accumulation of these factors would be strongly indicative.

ACCEPTANCE

For a successful, confident, and assertive leader, it is tempting to see failure as the result of others' negligence or mistakes and to believe that poor performance merely calls for redoubled courage and persistence. But such beliefs are often self-deceiving and even delusional. It is therefore important that leaders rely on more than just their own impressions. Advice can come from a variety of sources: the full board, selected directors, or, as in O'Neal's case, outside consultants.

ANALYSIS AND UNDERSTANDING

Once you recognize that Act II has arrived and that it requires a new type of leadership, the next step is to understand the nature of the shift. What would an Act II of your own making look like, and what are its implications for your leadership approach? An objective evaluation is often beneficial.

DECISION AND ACTION

I've seen CEOs employ a number of different strategies at this stage:

Personal change. In some cases, the CEO is able to step back, understand the requirements of Act II, and adjust his approach accordingly, as Stan O'Neal did. However, this modest-sounding goal requires a rare ability to reflect on one's own behavior and a willingness to reveal one's weaknesses and admit shortcomings. Then the leader must take on the task of self-transformation with all the determination and tenacity he formerly directed at pushing the organization forward. A CEO who can do that will no longer be the captive of strategies that have outlived their usefulness.

Structural change. Page and Brin's handoff to Schmidt can be seen as a classic case of redesigning the management structure to complement the strengths of the top people. Hewlett-Packard's board appears to have attempted the same thing with Fiorina. The board recognized the need for a change in leadership style and initially proposed not to remove Fiorina but to put in place a structure that would devolve some of her duties to subordinates better suited to overseeing day-to-day management. Fiorina, by most reports, rejected this approach, asserting that her own leadership style was best suited to institutionalizing the changes she had initiated.

Accelerated succession. Finally, a leader can acknowledge that the shift has begun and that it will call for a different chief executive. Such a decision requires a high degree of self- and situational awareness.

Many CEOs suffer from a misplaced sense of obligation to stick it out and complete the mission, even when signs are plentiful that hanging around would actually imperil it. Frankly, in 30 years of working with CEOs, I've hardly ever come across an occasion in which people thought the CEO had chosen to leave prematurely. The consensus is usually that the CEO has stuck around too long.

A SMART BOARD and a thorough search process will often turn up the right person to solve the company's immediate problems. But today's marketplace, in which buying patterns can suddenly shift and new technologies can materialize out of nowhere, will surely test a new CEO before long. Removing a maladaptive CEO before his time is messy and traumatizing for all concerned, including the ranks of employees. Consequently, boards have a duty to choose and cultivate leaders who can negotiate the transition from the first act to the second and, for that matter, from the second to the third, and so on. Moreover, boards can make sure that up-and-coming executives develop an awareness of, and receive training for, Act II transitions, so that if and when the individuals get to the C-suite, they are potentially more adaptive. Boards can do this by seeing to it that promising executives rotate through various locations, functions, and businesses; after all, divisions and subsidiaries present their top managers with Act IIs that are similar to, if less wrenching than, the crises that face corporate CEOs.

Such an approach expresses the ideal. In reality, there's a scarcity of CEOs who can repeatedly refashion themselves. The board therefore must respect the limitations of the mere mortal who has served the company well, if only for a few years. By the same token, proud CEOs must come to recognize when their time has passed.

Implications for the Board

THE NEAR INEVITABILITY that a new CEO will face an Act II that puts his or her skills and assumptions to a severe test places special responsibility in the hands of boards of directors. This advice is addressed to them.

- In succession and selection, beware of stylized leaders or one-trick ponies who seem to have succeeded in one kind of situation but have had limited exposure to a range of leadership challenges. Look for evidence that the individual has developed or could adopt more than one leadership approach.
- Pay attention to the possible leading indicators of CEO ineffectiveness, such as failure to deliver on promises, excessive rationalization of failures, departures of valued executives, or the CEO's seeming out of touch with his organization or even his own team. Often, a CEO's inability to adjust to a new set of issues reveals itself only when problems become acute. By then, it may be too late to do anything other than remove him. The board should collect data with an eye toward determining the CEO's ongoing effectiveness. The board's sense of his progress should be shared with the CEO and the company's other leaders.
- Recognize that the board has a role to play in mentoring and coaching the CEO. Too often, the board takes a

hands-off approach until it becomes apparent that the CEO is faltering.

- When faced with a crisis, recognize that you may need to think about a two-stage succession process. Consider bringing in a CEO specifically to handle the immediate problems. Make clear that once the crisis has been resolved, you may look for another CEO, one who is better suited to dealing with the next round of issues.

Originally published in January 2007
Reprint R0701F

Moments of Truth

Global Executives Talk About the Challenges That Shaped Them as Leaders

Executive Summary

WHEN DID YOU REALIZE you had the right stuff to lead? HBR's editors put that question to a group of business leaders representing different industries, nationalities, executive tenures, and company sizes. The answers were as diverse as the group itself.

Nokia CEO Olli-Pekka Kallasvuo recounts a lesson in humility, learned when he was a young CFO and it wasn't clear each month that the company would be able to pay salaries the next. Gary Jackson describes the challenge of preserving his military-training company's high-energy culture, largely through his own example. Arthur Gensler's story highlights the importance of vision in growing his architectural firm and refusing to be constrained by the traditions of a hidebound industry.

A world away, Alexander Cummings tells the harrowing tale of withstanding quarter after quarter of declining margins and market share—and intense pressure from his boss, and his boss's boss—because he had conviction that a controversial decision he made at Coca-Cola Africa would prove right in the end. Roche CEO Franz Humer recounts how he learned to trust his intuition, particularly when the rest of his organization was inclined to see only the downside risk in a deal.

Other leaders' moments of truth involved tests of still different qualities. Duleep Aluwihare of Ernst & Young in Poland learned from painful encounters with a mentor in his old firm, Arthur Andersen, that he must change his leadership style. Sergey Petrov, the founder of Russia's largest car importer, developed the perspective required of a leader when he was a young dissident held for questioning by the KGB. Finally, Alan Klapmeier of private-aircraft manufacturer Cirrus Design tells of the passion required to bring something truly innovative to market despite recalcitrant board members and the catastrophic loss of a prototype.

When did you realize you had the right stuff to lead? The answer depends, of course, on what you consider the right stuff to be. Is vision the essential quality of leadership? Is it the courage to act with conviction? Or does it have more to do with having passion, good instincts, or humility? The editors of *Harvard Business Review* asked business leaders in a variety of settings to tell us what they think is the most important leadership quality and how they've personally been tested. We didn't always get the story we expected.

It's easy to assume that leaders' stories mirror their organizations' travails and triumphs. If a company has suffered a highly visible setback—like a product recall or

a proxy fight—it seems obvious that the incident must have tested the chief executive's mettle. Likewise, when a company is known for a quality, like innovation or focus, we expect to see it reflected in the leader's own career. In contexts like these, leaders do show us what they're made of. But more often in the pages that follow, what we see is something they learned about themselves at a less public, more pivotal moment.

Humility

***Olli-Pekka Kallasvuo** has been the president and CEO of the telecommunications company Nokia, in Espoo, Finland, since June 2006.*

In 1990, I was 36 years old and had just been appointed chief financial officer at Nokia. It was a challenge—and not only because I was young. It was a turbulent time in the company's history. Nokia, which was already very big, was in quite a serious financial situation, and each month brought fears that we would not be able to pay salaries the next. What I also see now is how inexperienced I was, having come from a legal and strategy, rather than an accounting, background. There were many trips in those months—to Zurich, Frankfurt, Tokyo, London—while I tried to raise money from bankers who were losing faith as earnings continued to fall. Those long flights brought me face-to-face with the difficulty of our situation and how utterly alone I was. They changed me. Even when things got better financially, I knew where I stood, personally.

Humility is a vital quality in a leader, just as it is for a company. Nokia, if it is to continue to prosper, has to be externally oriented. It must have the kind of humility that makes it listen to the customer and seek ideas from outside. It has to be humble in the face of complexity. Especially today, as the convergence of mobility and the Internet has everyone guessing, Nokia can't be so overconfident as to believe its predictions are the best. Instead, we need to perceive changes as they occur and react the fastest. In a management team, that responsiveness is a product of diversity—managers must humbly accept that their own perspectives need to be broadened by others'.

Having humility does not mean that you are quiet or that you lack the courage to say what you think. Courage and humility are more complementary than contradictory. People who have been humbled by being down and out can have more courage when things get tough. They've been there already, and they understand that things are not always easy. But having humility does mean that you put your own contribution in perspective. It means that you know, as CEO, that your role is really to serve the company.

The demands on corporate leaders are so great, many CEOs come to understand that if they aren't committed to their jobs 101% they will not make it. For me, the realization came in the mid-1990s, when I worked abroad for two years. I made the decision that this is the life I am going to lead. I'm serving the company, and I will give it my all.

When you have made that decision, you grow as a person. It gives you the courage to speak up when everyone in a room says, "This is the case," and you don't agree. It gives you the strength to resist the safe conformity of benchmarking and instead try to think differently. It allows you (in fact, compels you) to say that things have changed, and we need to change, too.

At the same time, that perspective makes you appreciate how much you depend on others—another humbling realization. When I was first put in charge of a team 19 years ago, I had to come to terms with the fact that I was no longer a lone professional doing my own job. I had to manage in such a way that other people would be the ones making things happen, not me. With every year, the lesson has intensified. As of January 2007, Nokia has 100,000 people, and there's really very little I can do alone. But there is much I can do with the team.

Energy

Gary Jackson *(gjackson@blackwaterusa.com) is the president of Blackwater USA, a private military contractor and security firm based in Moyock, North Carolina.*

THE CRUCIAL TURNING POINT in the fortunes of Blackwater USA occurred in the wake of the October 2000 bombing of the USS *Cole.* Suddenly, the U.S. Navy urgently needed the type of training we provide. In fact, the Navy asked us to train 20,000 sailors in six months at facilities in four locations. Our company at that point consisted of 30 people. I remember thinking, "Oh my goodness." But I had no qualms about saying yes. We had it all, even if we hadn't put it all together. Before those six months were up, the nation suffered the terrorist attacks of September 11, and Blackwater was growing from a small training center into a major force.

The key to our growth has been our culture. Almost as soon as you set foot on the 7,000-acre campus at our North Carolina headquarters, you feel the energy of the place. Some of this is just a function of who we are. A lot of our people are from Special Ops—Green Berets and Navy SEALs. These are people who, when presented with a challenge, don't say "Hmmm." They say, "Let's go." But it's also a function of how we choose to run things. I've tried to take the best of military culture and structure (I might be the only corporate president who has a corporate master chief and a chaplain reporting to him) and keep the chain of command short, so bureaucracy doesn't overtake us.

To keep the spirit entrepreneurial, I sponsor "100-day projects." Anyone at any level in the company who has an idea for making or saving money is given free rein to pursue it, so long as the payoff can be realized within 100 days. We've got six of those projects running at the moment.

Everyone who knows me knows about the personal database I keep. I've got 3,500 names tagged with either a "T" or a "D," depending on whether the person is a talker or a doer. I constantly push for the 80% solution that is executable now over the 100% solution we might be able to devise in another three weeks.

Our culture is what has made our name as a company, and the biggest test I face as a leader is preserving it. Some of that test comes down to personal behavior. In our parking lot, we have only one spot marked "reserved," but it's reserved for the first person who gets to work in the morning. More often than not, I get it. One of the challenges of working in a super-energy environment is that the company feels it when the leader is flagging. I can't slow down.

The greater part of the test comes with high-profile decisions, especially about personnel. Six weeks ago, I had to make a wrenching one regarding a dozen people who were hired way back when I was just getting staff on board. They had developed that 100% solution mentality, wanting to form working groups that would discuss possibilities for weeks. That isn't us. But I wrestled with the decision because another huge part of our culture is loyalty. We have 6,000 men and women working in nine very dangerous countries, plus another 1,000 in the U.S., and they do it because they love the company. But they also do it because I've said that their loyalty will be returned. Most have families, and we make their well-being our business, too. When I asked those dozen people to leave, I risked sending the wrong kind of signal about Blackwater. But I knew it was the right thing to do: I'd already let them stay longer than was good for the company.

In the 23 years I spent as a Navy SEAL, my leadership capabilities were tested at every step. I had to prove I could lead two or three people, then 16 people, and so on into the hundreds. Today, I'm an entrepreneur leading a 7,000-man force that believes in doing what it says it will do and at speeds that nobody can believe. My job is to keep that going.

Intuition

Franz Humer *is the chairman and CEO of the pharmaceutical firm Roche, based in Basel, Switzerland.*

PEOPLE OFTEN TALK ABOUT the loneliness at the top of an organization. It's true: The balance is not easy to strike when you want to build and work in a team but must make difficult decisions that you cannot always share with the team members.

But leaders have to go it alone in another important way. Many times, when opportunities arise to grow the business or to make substantial changes, your internal organization talks to you only about the risks you run—about all the things that could go wrong. When the evidence presented to you is so unevenly stacked, it's up to you to know how much trust to have in the other side of the deal.

Sometimes, the resistance takes the form of unquestioned assumptions. In the mid-1990s, when I was with another company, we had an ulcer treatment that had reached £1 billion in sales—which was as much as any pharmaceutical product had ever sold. I believed sales could go twice as high, but convincing the marketing teams and general managers around the world was a huge challenge. The whole organization was absolutely convinced it couldn't be done. Why? Simply because it hadn't been done before.

Often, the resistance has better arguments than that. I remember the debates four years ago when Roche bought the majority interest in a Japanese company. It was established wisdom that one could not acquire a Japanese company and be successful. Western companies that had tried had never really been recognized as Japanese players in Japan, as opposed to foreigners coming in. It is true that, given how business is done there, it is difficult to understand and navigate the marketplace, especially if you don't speak the language. It was also true that Roche already had a market presence in Japan under our own brand name. As part of the deal, we would be giving that up, integrating the operations, management, and products into those of the Japanese company. My colleagues weren't at all confident that it was worthwhile to walk away from what had been built over 75 years.

Today, Chugai Pharmaceutical is one of the top three players in the world's second largest pharmaceutical market. But four years ago, I had to trust it would work. I did, in large part, because I trusted my counterpart in the negotiations. Our relationship had developed over a five-year period in which we had started discussions, then broken them off, then come back together. Usually, a leader has less to go on yet still must make the decision on how much to trust.

How does one learn that judgment? It's a matter of becoming hyperaware of your environment and learning to sense the vibe in the room. Especially in a negotiation setting, I try to have my entire body, my entire mind, all my emotions switched on to "receiving." How are people reacting? How are they behaving? If you can enter this mode, you can be sensitive to small changes that other people wouldn't even notice. Perhaps I've developed some of that sensitivity from living in many different countries and speaking many different languages. By now, with no strong roots in any given culture, I gravitate quickly to what is common to all people.

The pharmaceutical business is filled with licensing deals, business development partnerships, and product alliances. For any significant deal, I insist on meeting with the other people before we sign. I want to know with whom we are dealing. And I have walked away from deals when I have felt I cannot trust those people.

This does not take the form of some dramatic scene. Rather, I go back and take a closer look at the deal, then, perhaps, realize that the risk is a little too high, the terms are a little too loose, or there is a bit too much flexibility. I'm a lawyer by training, so if trust is not there, I want to have everything nailed down to the last iota. The Japanese deal was a mere two-page document that my counterpart and I signed. We gave it to the lawyers and financial people and said, "This is what you need to make happen."

Vision

Arthur Gensler *founded Gensler—a global architecture, design, planning, and consulting firm—41 years ago. The firm has grown to 2,400 people in 30 offices.*

IN 1965, I had just finished a major project for San Francisco's BART public transit system, setting the standards—down to how many restrooms were needed—for 13 teams who were designing 33 stations. I was working for the architectural firm of Wurster, Bernardi & Emmons, under the legendary William Wurster, who had formerly been dean of the architecture schools at both Berkeley and MIT. He encouraged me (as he did everyone) to hang out my own shingle.

It happened around that time that I met up with an old college classmate one night, and he told me he needed help in tenant development work. This involved meeting with potential tenants of an office building and drawing up plans for how they would fit into the facility. It's what's known as space planning today, but back then it was considered below the dignity of a "real" architect. Typically, an office manager or furniture dealer would sketch out the floor plan on graph paper. What passed for interior design was putting a few Barcelona chairs in a lobby.

My friend was the development manager for a San Francisco waterfront project called the Golden Gateway, which included the Alcoa building, a major new office tower. The conversation intrigued me. I thought in this "tenant work" there might be the makings of a valuable business.

So I rented some space and four drafting tables, hired one draftsman, and took my friend up on his offer. It wasn't the best time to take an entrepreneurial risk. I had a wife and three children to support, and a total of $200 in savings. I can't claim I had any business acumen. There's virtually no business training in architecture school. But I listened to the people in the legal, finance, and consulting companies who were the tenants. I asked about what they did and how they worked. I became fascinated with the way organizations operate in a space. And I soon realized that there was an opportunity to professionalize tenant work, to thoughtfully analyze the space requirements of the various business functions and raise that to a new level of service.

To understand how different this client-based perspective was, consider one of the oldest lines in the profession: "I could do a great project if it weren't for the client." It's always said jokingly, but architects really do refer to projects as *their* buildings when in fact the buildings belong to the clients. I came to see that architecture is all about the user of the building. It isn't just what you see as you drive down the street; it's about the environment we create inside.

In the following decades, we continued to question traditional industry practices. We put in a profit-sharing plan and created in-house management-training courses. We adopted a structure based on practice areas. Most successful firms still operate on a project basis, which means a lot of hiring and firing to match the workload and no interest in small jobs. Our structure allows us to welcome both large and small projects, as long as the work is for a quality client. I remember loaning a single draftsman to someone for a small project 35 years ago. That was Don Fisher, who was opening his second Gap store, and we've worked with him ever since.

The most important decision we made was to do away with the star system: Outside Gensler, the profession is still very much centered on a "name" architect.

But a hugely complex project cannot hinge on one person. It takes a star to get the project, a star to design the project, a star to document the design, a star to build it, a star to collect fees, and a star to run the business behind them. We've built a team culture where we are all stars, no matter what role we play on a project.

By 1995, "Gensler and Associates, Architects" had evolved to the point where we were offering many different services besides tenant planning—architecture, consulting, brand strategy, product design, master planning, and interior design. Perhaps I shouldn't have been surprised when our branding and graphics group suggested that we take "architects" out of our name. It no longer defined the broad consultative practice we had become. Still, it was an agonizing decision for me. Like most people in the profession, I think design is in my blood. At the age of five, I told people I would grow up to be an architect, and at Cornell's Department of Architecture I won the top award in my graduating class. My profession is central to my identity.

But I've discovered there are always new ways to define the profession. Recently we have started a new kind of service for very large-scale, complex projects. We are managing the designs of six other world-renowned architects, as well as providing our own design services, for MGM Mirage in Las Vegas. It is an unprecedented role within the industry, and there was no term for it. We've settled on "executive architect."

Perspective

Sergey Petrov *(sapetrov@rolf.ru) is the founder and sole owner of the $2.4 billion Rolf Group, Russia's largest foreign car importer and distributor.*

My professional life began in the military, and by 26, I was a major in command of a squadron. So one could say that I was benefiting personally from the Communist system, but still it made me sick. By 1982, unrest had flared up in Poland in the form of the Solidarnost movement, and a group of friends and I felt that mass protest could develop along similar lines here. We began to meet, to study market economies and the history of Western democracies, to analyze the flaws of the Soviet system, and to talk about Russia's future. We felt that it was necessary to prepare training courses for people who might lead the trade union movement. It was when we started to print flyers that the KGB took notice, as we knew it eventually would. But when you see that something is wrong, you have a choice: Either you convince yourself that everything's all right and become a moral invalid, or you resist.

When I was first held for questioning, the counterintelligence chief of the Volga Military Administrative District, a General Dan'kov, said to me, "So you, Major, want us to have democracy? But here, everything is for the people. I'll tell you what: Why don't I bring you to the nearest factory and tell the workers, 'This man wants everything to be like in America.' They will tear you to pieces." I thought to myself, "It really might be better to go home to my wife." He was right that I'd be going to jail for people who had become so used to slavery that they didn't question it—even loved it.

It's difficult for most people to see the system they are part of for what it is, and perhaps that is one test of a leader. The same lack of perspective often keeps people from seeing how their own mentality might be a constraint. After the company I founded, Rolf, began growing rapidly in the 1990s, I had to recognize how the attitudes of some of my Russian executives were creating risks they didn't perceive. In late 2000, for example, we were supposed to pay an Austrian construction firm several million dollars on a contract it had already completed. But just as the payment was coming due, there was a change in Russian customs regulations, which led to an upsurge in demand for cars. To satisfy it, we had to import many more vehicles than originally planned. "Can we find the money?" I asked my finance director. "Yes," he said, "if we hold back from paying the Austrians." I called and negotiated one month's grace. But somehow, three months went by, and the bill was still not paid. In my finance director's mind, it was a matter of "So what? It's only a small fine for being overdue." He had no notion that it wouldn't be seen this way in other parts of the world, where a lag in payment is considered a default and a catastrophe. Rumors, in fact, were already flying.

After that, I told him, "Listen, man, I love you very much, and I'm ready to go dancing or fishing with you, but I'm going to hand over the finances to someone else—someone whose mentality corresponds to that of our foreign partners." That turned out to be Matt Donnelly, the Irishman I recently made CEO of the business.

The emphasis we put on our reputation has paid off. Last year, for example, we were able to get $350 million under favorable terms from a syndicate of Western banks, saving us the astronomical interest we would have paid in Russia.

Over the years, I've had to put a great deal of effort into defending the foreign executives I've brought in. Our Russian managers are ambitious guys; they know what life is all about, and suddenly they have to obey a foreigner who seems to know nothing. His Russian is terrible, and his own language incomprehensible. And, in truth, foreigners can be pretty strange: They try to rally people around HR technologies and other programs that really don't work here. But we need to have our perspectives challenged. So when emotions have run too high, I've said, "That's it. Stop! If you can't work with them, we'll just have to replace you!"

It's one thing to manage a $10 million company and another thing to manage one that has grown into the billions. You need a different approach, and not everyone can make the transition. When I've recognized that and made management changes along the way, people have become upset. "Why did you do this," they've asked me, "when everything was going well? There was no decline in the numbers. . . ." But you can't sit around waiting to go into decline. If you can see the limitations in a situation, you can act to transcend them.

Passion

***Alan Klapmeier** cofounded Cirrus Design, a Duluth, Minnesota–based manufacturer of private aircraft, with his brother, Dale, in 1984.*

IN THE MID-1980S, I was flying with an instructor and had a midair collision with another small airplane. We were barely able to land safely, and I watched the other guy hit the ground. It turned out to be a friend of mine from the next airport over who died. I was passionate about flying before that—my brother, Dale, and I had been airplane nuts from boyhood. But after that day, I was passionate about airplane safety.

That's probably why, when a company called Ballistic Recovery Systems developed a workable full-plane parachute, we were the one aircraft maker interested. Our company, Cirrus Design, was just beginning to make a name for itself in the industry; the guys from BRS had already called on everyone else. When we said yes, they almost couldn't believe it—but it fit in perfectly with what we were trying to do.

If you talk to people who like to fly but aren't pilots, you tend to hear a common refrain. "I've always wanted to learn, but it's so *expensive,*" they say—as they climb into their Lexus and head off to golf at the country club. It's an excuse, because they don't want to admit that either it's too hard or they're afraid. Private-aircraft designers need to address the fear in two ways: by changing people's perceptions—because flying is really a lot safer than most people think—and by changing the reality—because it's also more dangerous than it could be. A parachute on the airplane helps do both. And so does another innovation we brought to market: a more intuitive panel flight display.

The argument for the new PFD—what the industry now calls the "glass cockpit"—is straightforward. Pilots are much more prone to accidents when they're using instrument flight rules (IFR), when visibility is limited, than when they're using visual flight rules (VFR), on a clear day. Those who've made mistakes usually say they got into trouble when they "broke their scan." The scan is the routine way pilots learn to watch the round gauges in front of them and keep their bearings: They look at the artificial horizon, then at the airspeed, then back to the artificial horizon, then at the altitude, then back to the artificial horizon, then at the heading—and back to the beginning. That constant reference back to the artificial horizon is necessary because it's the only way to know which way is up when the natural horizon is not visible. If some distraction in the cockpit (maybe as minor as having to fiddle with radio knobs) makes you break the scan, you can easily become very disoriented.

Pilots use the same gauges flying VFR. But if they break their scan, they rarely get into trouble because they have information coming in from the corner of their eye to alert them to a change in their attitude. What we realized is that computer technology could replace the quaint little gauge with an artificial horizon spanning the width of the cockpit. That edge-to-edge image, mounted horizontally instead of vertically, is similar to being able to see the actual horizon. Combine that with a big, moving map, and the new PFD relieves the pilot of having to spend so much energy just forming a mental picture of what the plane is doing. The pilot becomes less a data collector and more a decision maker. Bottom line: It's safer.

But as logical as it seems, this innovation would never have made it to market if we hadn't been truly passionate about it. When we went to air shows and told people about the features we were designing and how they would change the industry, people laughed at us—literally. My own board of directors tried to stop me from introducing it. In their defense, we had just spent $100,000 doing a market research study and, of all the product development ideas the respondents weighed in on, that one ranked dead last. But I said, "You can't ask a question of somebody who doesn't understand the question and make a decision based upon their answer. They don't know how good this stuff is going to be—how it will change the way they fly, change safety, change utility. They're just wrong." I knew I was betting the company, and I said so. I also knew it would be my head if it didn't work.

I made things even harder for myself by insisting that this great new technology would be standard on all our airplanes, including our base model. I knew other people thought it should be a high-priced option—but my thinking was the complete opposite, that it had to be for entry-level aircraft owners because, by making it easier for them, we'd keep them in the game.

Anyone who's passionate about the future of general aviation should see it this way: When it's easier to fly, people fly more often, and when they fly more often, they find they get better value out of flying—and they stick with it. That benefits the whole industry. The attitude of some pilots amazes me. I remember one complaining to me after a presentation I did at the Oshkosh air show in the mid-1990s. "If you do all the stuff you're talking about," he said, "then *anybody* will be able to fly." I said, "Yeah, that's the idea!"

You have to have passion to do something industry changing—and not only because there are so many skeptics. You also need it to get you through all the setbacks. In so many businesses, there's a tendency anytime something goes wrong to abandon the whole approach and go in another direction. There's not enough passion, or perseverance, or conviction that the basic idea is right. People shrug and say, "Well, that didn't work. Let's go and do something different," as opposed to, "Well, that didn't work, but *what about it* didn't work?"

Not long after we started Cirrus Design, we faced that kind of moment. It was a week before Oshkosh, and we were testing a prototype of our first airplane. I did the test flight with one of the engineers, Dean Vogel, in the right seat. My brother and our chief engineer were in the chase airplane. As one of the guys closed up the engine compartment, he asked me if I wanted to wait while he put in some new fire extinguishers. The airplane had automatic fire protection, but the fire protection bottles had blown off the day before when the engine overheated. I said "No, they'll just blow off again." I was saving $25 worth of fire extinguishers.

It was right after takeoff that the chase airplane came alongside, and I heard the chief engineer yelling, "Fire! Fire! Fire!" We set the plane down in a field about a mile off the runway, got out, and proceeded to watch it burn. Afterwards we gathered everybody together, maybe 20 of us, and went to the local Pizza Hut. "The *good* news," I said, "is that it burned up completely—because think how much work we'd have to do this week if it were only damaged." Everybody kind of laughed, and then we talked about how to get back on track. As we were leaving, someone said, "I can't believe it; I just assumed we were out of business. I mean, we lost the prototype." We said, "No, we still believe we're right. There's a market here, and we understand the technology. We're going to make this work."

Conviction

***Alexander B. Cummings** (acummings@eur.ko.com) is the president and chief operating officer of the Coca-Cola Company's Africa Group. He is based in Windsor, UK.*

WHEN YOU ARE A LEADER, but not *the* leader, of an enterprise, the tests of your ability come as strongly from above as they do from below. Early in my days with Coca-Cola Africa, I made a decision that I felt was a good one at the time, but unfortunately the short-term results were not proving me right. Quite the contrary, my judgment was costing the company volume and market share. I remember feeling intense pressure to reverse the decision and stem the losses.

Here was the situation: The Coca-Cola Company was at the time, as it still is, a very competitive enterprise. Volume and share growth was paramount; we wanted to see continuous increases in the per capita consumption of our products. But I saw a situation where that focus was taking a toll on the overall health of our business system, especially for our indispensable partners—our bottlers.

In a market with high inflation and currency devaluation, we had held price for several years to maintain our growth momentum. As a result, our bottler was struggling to make adequate returns. In the interest of overall system profitability, I made the unpopular decision to increase prices. I firmly believed that it was the right decision to serve our own company's long-term interests, even though the primary beneficiary of the price increase was the bottler. After much debate, I got agreement to proceed with the controversial, yet vital, price increase.

We all knew that the decision would lead to a decline in volumes—but I hadn't anticipated how dramatically they would drop. Even more worrisome, despite the fact that our competitor followed suit and raised its own prices within a few weeks, we were also losing market share. The pressure began mounting.

I was an experienced manager, having come from a company where I had served as CFO for the international business. But until that point in my career, I can honestly say I had never felt so much pressure to reverse a decision—to roll back prices. I was in somewhat of a quandary; I would be putting my career at risk if the declines in volume and market share persisted.

Despite the pressure, I was convinced that in the medium to long term, the decision would prove to be the right one, both for the company and our bottler. We just needed the fortitude to ride out the short-term effects. I knew, too, that my leadership and credibility—as well as any future influence—with the bottler would be severely damaged if I retracted my decision. Finally, I trusted my instincts and knew that my company was in fact paying me to make calls like this.

Fortunately, things did work out in the end. After six tough months, the declines finally bottomed out. In the fourth quarter, the bottler began to see the financial benefits. Ultimately, our economics changed for the better, as well. Today, even though we have some challenges in that market, the system continues to benefit from that decision. And just as I underestimated the short-term negative effects, I also underestimated how much our relationship with the bottler would also change for the better. People there had expected me to cave in under the pressure. But once I held my ground, it was the beginning of a whole new chapter. Not only did the economics of the relationship shift but so did the psychology. We at the Coca-Cola Company had demonstrated that we understood the bottler's challenges and were supportive of them. In the eyes of that important business partner, and for my growth as a leader, seeing this tough decision through was indeed a defining moment.

Learning

***Duleep Aluwihare** is the managing partner at the accounting firm Ernst & Young in Warsaw, Poland.*

THE MOST DIFFICULT experience in my business career came with the collapse of Arthur Andersen, a company at which I had worked for 25 years, and one that was once the leader in the consulting market. The demise of Andersen was a traumatic experience not only for me but also for 800 workers of Andersen in Poland. We did survive; almost every consultant from Andersen transferred to Ernst & Young. I was able to keep the team intact and maintain the trust of our clients in the Polish consulting market.

This might not have been the case had I not previously undergone a difficult personal development experience that improved my managerial abilities. When I came to Poland in 1989 from London, where I had worked for Andersen since I'd graduated from the London School of Economics, my job was to build the Polish Andersen office from scratch. After a few years, we were achieving great results and developing a client base more rapidly than our competitors.

Unfortunately, our success went to my head. Totally subconsciously, I grew to have a stronger and stronger feeling of my own infallibility. My friends say that I became arrogant. I was terrifically self-confident; I felt sure that I could do everything. I even bought a Jaguar—a car that not many people in Poland drove at that time.

I received a visit from my mentor, Manuel Soto, a creator of the Spanish Andersen, who was supervising the activity of the company in Europe. Manuel observed my behavior at work and said that as a company director I had strayed from the right leadership path. I listened to him, of course, but without conviction.

Not long afterwards, our biggest client failed to pay us for two major deals. The loss caused me to lose face; I had to explain myself to my bosses. Manuel took one look at me and scolded me: "Look what arrogance leads to. You pretended to be a superman; you were sure you could do anything. And now you're asking us for understanding and forgiveness." He told me I had to change. I had to stop showing off and trying to dominate people. I had to regain their respect. I had to rebuild the trust of others in me as a leader and support them during good and bad times. He added that I shouldn't overestimate the strength of personal involvement in the daily work of the team, because success springs from the team's work.

This time I took the lesson to heart; I adopted a completely different leadership model. I tried to become an example for others. I set very high standards for myself, and I expected everyone to do likewise. I stopped simply giving instructions, and I worked on the front line with my people. I tried to build a culture in which the employees could make decisions quickly and would not be afraid of challenges and possible failures.

The personal and behavioral changes the team and I both made stood us in good stead when Andersen was in trouble. Suddenly, everything my coworkers and I had spent so many years building was about to fall apart. My leadership was put to the test. I didn't know how many people would stay with me or how many would trust me during the hardest months, when we were negotiating the merger with E&Y and our competitors were trying to buy our consultants. We managed, however, to emerge victorious from that trial, and today E&Y Poland is doing well.

And as for the Jaguar . . . that problem was solved, too. The car was stolen.

Originally published in January 2007
Reprint R0701A

How Leaders Create and Use Networks

HERMINIA IBARRA AND MARK HUNTER

Executive Summary

MOST PEOPLE ACKNOWLEDGE that networking–creating a fabric of personal contacts to provide support, feedback, insight, and resources–is an essential activity for an ambitious manager. Indeed, it's a requirement even for those focused simply on doing their current jobs well. For some, this is a distasteful reality. Working through networks, they believe, means relying on "who you know" rather than "what you know"– a hypocritical, possibly unethical, way to get things done. But even people who understand that networking is a legitimate and necessary part of their jobs can be discouraged by the payoff–because they are doing it in too limited a fashion.

On the basis of a close study of 30 emerging leaders, the authors outline three distinct forms of networking. *Operational* networking is geared toward doing one's assigned tasks more effectively. It involves cultivating stronger relationships with colleagues whose membership in the network is clear; their roles define them as stakeholders. *Personal* networking engages kindred spirits from outside an organization in an individual's efforts to learn and find opportunities for personal advancement. *Strategic* networking puts the tools of networking in the service of business goals. At this level, a manager creates the kind of network that will help uncover and capitalize on new opportunities for the company. The ability to move to this level of networking turns out to be a key test of leadership.

Companies often recognize that networks are valuable, and they create explicit programs to support them. But typically these programs facilitate only operational networking. Likewise, industry associations provide formal contexts for personal networking. The unfortunate effect is to give managers the impression that they know how to network and are doing so sufficiently. A sidebar notes the implication for companies' leadership development initiatives: that teaching strategic networking skills will serve their aspiring leaders and their business goals well.

WHEN HENRIK BALMER became the production manager and a board member of a newly bought-out cosmetics firm, improving his network was the last thing on his mind. The main problem he faced was time: Where would he find the hours to guide his team through a major upgrade of the production process and then think about strategic issues like expanding the business? The only way he could carve out time and still get

home to his family at a decent hour was to lock himself—literally—in his office. Meanwhile, there were day-to-day issues to resolve, like a recurring conflict with his sales director over custom orders that compromised production efficiency. Networking, which Henrik defined as the unpleasant task of trading favors with strangers, was a luxury he could not afford. But when a new acquisition was presented at a board meeting without his input, he abruptly realized he was out of the loop—not just inside the company, but outside, too—at a moment when his future in the company was at stake.

Henrik's case is not unusual. Over the past two years, we have been following a cohort of 30 managers making their way through what we call the leadership transition, an inflection point in their careers that challenges them to rethink both themselves and their roles. In the process, we've found that networking—creating a fabric of personal contacts who will provide support, feedback, insight, resources, and information—is simultaneously one of the most self-evident and one of the most dreaded developmental challenges that aspiring leaders must address.

Their discomfort is understandable. Typically, managers rise through the ranks by dint of a strong command of the technical elements of their jobs and a nose-to-the-grindstone focus on accomplishing their teams' objectives. When challenged to move beyond their functional specialties and address strategic issues facing the overall business, many managers do not immediately grasp that this will involve relational—not analytical—tasks. Nor do they easily understand that exchanges and interactions with a diverse array of current and potential stakeholders are not distractions from their "real work" but are actually at the heart of their new leadership roles.

Like Henrik (whose identity we've disguised, along with all the other managers we describe here), a majority of the managers we work with say that they find networking insincere or manipulative—at best, an elegant way of using people. Not surprisingly, for every manager who instinctively constructs and maintains a useful network, we see several who struggle to overcome this innate resistance. Yet the alternative to networking is to fail—either in reaching for a leadership position or in succeeding at it.

Watching our emerging leaders approach this daunting task, we discovered that three distinct but interdependent forms of networking—*operational, personal,* and *strategic*—played a vital role in their transitions. The first helped them manage current internal responsibilities, the second boosted their personal development, and the third opened their eyes to new business directions and the stakeholders they would need to enlist. While our managers differed in how well they pursued operational and personal networking, we discovered that almost all of them underutilized strategic networking. In this article, we describe key features of each networking form (summarized in the exhibit "The Three Forms of Networking") and, using our managers' experiences, explain how a three-pronged networking strategy can become part and parcel of a new leader's development plan.

Operational Networking

All managers need to build good working relationships with the people who can help them do their jobs. The number and breadth of people involved can be impressive—such operational networks include not only direct reports and superiors but also peers within an

The Three Forms of Networking

Managers who think they are adept at networking are often operating only at an operational or personal level. Effective leaders learn to employ networks for strategic purposes.

	Operational	Personal	Strategic
Purpose	Getting work done efficiently; maintaining the capacities and functions required of the group.	Enhancing personal and professional development; providing referrals to useful information and contacts.	Figuring out future priorities and challenges; getting stakeholder support for them.
Location and temporal orientation	Contacts are mostly internal and oriented toward current demands.	Contacts are mostly external and oriented toward current interests and future potential interests.	Contacts are internal and external and oriented toward the future.
Players and recruitment	Key contacts are relatively nondiscretionary; they are prescribed mostly by the task and organizational structure, so it is very clear who is relevant.	Key contacts are mostly discretionary; it is not always clear who is relevant.	Key contacts follow from the strategic context and the organizational environment, but specific membership is discretionary; it is not always clear who is relevant.
Network attributes and key behaviors	Depth: building strong working relationships.	Breadth: reaching out to contacts who can make referrals.	Leverage: creating inside-outside links.

operational unit, other internal players with the power to block or support a project, and key outsiders such as suppliers, distributors, and customers. The purpose of this type of networking is to ensure coordination and cooperation among people who have to know and trust one another in order to accomplish their immediate tasks. That isn't always easy, but it is relatively straightforward, because the task provides focus and a clear criterion for membership in the network: Either you're necessary to the job and helping to get it done, or you're not.

Although operational networking was the form that came most naturally to the managers we studied, nearly every one had important blind spots regarding people and groups they depended on to make things happen. In one case, Alistair, an accounting manager who worked in an entrepreneurial firm with several hundred employees, was suddenly promoted by the company's founder to financial director and given a seat on the board. He was both the youngest and the least-experienced board member, and his instinctive response to these new responsibilities was to reestablish his functional credentials. Acting on a hint from the founder that the company might go public, Alistair undertook a reorganization of the accounting department that would enable the books to withstand close scrutiny. Alistair succeeded brilliantly in upgrading his team's capabilities, but he missed the fact that only a minority of the seven-person board shared the founder's ambition. A year into Alistair's tenure, discussion about whether to take the company public polarized the board, and he discovered that all that time cleaning up the books might have been better spent sounding out his codirectors.

One of the problems with an exclusive reliance on operational networks is that they are usually geared toward meeting objectives as assigned, not toward asking the strategic question, "What *should* we be doing?" By the same token, managers do not exercise as much personal choice in assembling operational relationships as they do in weaving personal and strategic networks, because to a large extent the right relationships are prescribed by the job and organizational structure. Thus, most operational networking occurs within an organization, and ties are determined in large part by routine, short-term demands. Relationships formed with outsiders, such as board members, customers, and regulators, are directly task-related and tend to be bounded and constrained by demands determined at a higher level. Of course, an individual manager can choose to deepen and develop the ties to different extents, and all managers exercise discretion over who gets priority attention. It's the quality of relationships—the rapport and mutual trust—that gives an operational network its power. Nonetheless, the substantial constraints on network membership mean these connections are unlikely to deliver value to managers beyond assistance with the task at hand.

The typical manager in our group was more concerned with sustaining cooperation within the existing network than with building relationships to face nonroutine or unforeseen challenges. But as a manager moves into a leadership role, his or her network must reorient itself externally and toward the future.

Personal Networking

We observed that once aspiring leaders like Alistair awaken to the dangers of an excessively internal focus, they begin to seek kindred spirits outside their organizations. Simultaneously, they become aware of the limitations of their social skills, such as a lack of knowledge about professional domains beyond their own, which makes it difficult for them to find common ground with people outside their usual circles. Through professional associations, alumni groups, clubs, and personal interest communities, managers gain new perspectives that allow them to advance in their careers. This is what we mean by personal networking.

Many of the managers we study question why they should spend precious time on an activity so indirectly related to the work at hand. Why widen one's circle of casual acquaintances when there isn't time even for urgent tasks? The answer is that these contacts provide important referrals, information, and, often, developmental support such as coaching and mentoring. A newly appointed factory director, for example, faced with a turnaround-or-close-down situation that was paralyzing his staff, joined a business organization—and through it met a lawyer who became his counsel in the turnaround. Buoyed by his success, he networked within his company's headquarters in search of someone who had dealt with a similar crisis. Eventually, he found two mentors.

A personal network can also be a safe space for personal development and as such can provide a foundation for strategic networking. The experience of Timothy, a principal in a midsize software company, is a good example. Like his father, Timothy stuttered. When he had the opportunity to prepare for meetings, his stutter was not an issue, but spontaneous encounters inside and outside the company were dreadfully painful. To solve this problem, he began accepting at least two invitations per week to the social gatherings he had assiduously ignored before. Before each event, he asked who else had been invited and did background research on the other guests so that he could initiate conversations. The hardest part, he said, was "getting through the door." Once inside, his interest in the conversations helped him forget himself and master his stutter. As his stutter diminished, he also applied himself to networking across his company, whereas previously he had taken refuge in his technical expertise. Like Timothy, several of our emerging leaders successfully used personal networking as a relatively safe way to expose problems and seek insight into solutions—safe, that is, compared with strategic networking, in which the stakes are far higher.

Personal networks are largely external, made up of discretionary links to people with whom we have something in common. As a result, what makes a personal network powerful is its referral potential. According to the famous six degrees of separation principle, our personal contacts are valuable to the extent that they help us reach, in as few connections as possible, the far-off person who has the information we need.

In watching managers struggle to widen their professional relationships in ways that feel both natural and legitimate to them, we repeatedly saw them shift their time and energy from operational to personal networking. For people who have rarely looked outside their organizations, this is an important first step, one that fosters a deeper understanding of themselves and the environments in which they move. Ultimately, however, personal networking alone won't propel managers through the leadership transition. Aspiring leaders may find people who awaken new interests but fail to become comfortable with the power players at the level above them. Or they may achieve new influence within a professional community but fail to harness those ties in the service of organizational goals. That's why managers who know they need to develop their networking skills, and make a real effort to do so, nonetheless may end up feeling like they have wasted their time and energy. As we'll see, personal networking will not help a manager through the leadership transition unless he or she learns how to bring those connections to bear on organizational strategy.

Strategic Networking

When managers begin the delicate transition from functional manager to business leader, they must start to concern themselves with broad strategic issues. Lateral and vertical relationships with other functional and business unit managers—all people outside their immediate control—become a lifeline for figuring out how their own contributions fit into the big picture. (See "From Functional Manager to Business Leader: How Companies Can Help" at the end of this article.) Thus strategic networking plugs the aspiring leader into a set of relationships and information sources that collectively embody the power to achieve personal and organizational goals.

Operating beside players with diverse affiliations, backgrounds, objectives, and incentives requires a manager to formulate business rather than functional objectives, and to work through the coalitions and networks needed to sell ideas and compete for resources. Consider Sophie, a manager who, after rising steadily through the ranks in logistics and distribution, was stupefied to learn that the CEO was considering a radical reorganization of her function that would strip her of some responsibilities. Rewarded to date for incremental annual improvements, she had failed to notice shifting priorities in the wider market and the resulting internal shuffle for resources and power at the higher levels of her company. Although she had built a loyal, high-performing team, she had few relationships outside her group to help her anticipate the new imperatives, let alone give her ideas about how to respond. After she argued that distribution issues were her purview, and failed to be persuasive, she hired consultants to help her prepare a counterproposal. But Sophie's boss simply concluded that she lacked a broad, longer-term business perspective. Frustrated, Sophie contemplated leaving the company. Only after some patient coaching from a senior manager did she understand that she had to get out of her unit and start talking to opinion leaders inside and outside the company to form a sellable plan for the future.

What differentiates a leader from a manager, research tells us, is the ability to figure out where to go and to enlist the people and groups necessary to get there. Recruiting stakeholders, lining up allies and sympathizers, diagnosing the political landscape, and brokering conversations among unconnected parties are all part of a leader's job. As they step up to the leadership transition, some managers accept their growing dependence on others and seek to transform it into mutual influence. Others dismiss such work as "political" and, as a result, undermine their ability to advance their goals.

Several of the participants in our sample chose the latter approach, justifying their choice as a matter of personal values and integrity. In one case, Jody, who managed a department in a large company under what she described as "dysfunctional" leadership, refused even to try to activate her extensive network within the firm when internal adversaries took over key functions of her unit. When we asked her why she didn't seek help from anyone in the organization to stop this coup, she replied that she refused to play "stupid political games. . . . You can only do what you think is the ethical and right thing from your perspective." Stupid or not, those games cost her the respect and support of her direct reports and coworkers, who hesitated to follow someone they perceived as unwilling to defend herself. Eventually she had no choice but to leave.

The key to a good strategic network is leverage: the ability to marshal information, support, and resources from one sector of a network to achieve results in another. Strategic networkers use indirect influence, convincing one person in the network to get someone else, who is not in the network, to take a needed action. Moreover, strategic networkers don't just influence their relational environment; they shape it in their own image by moving and hiring subordinates, changing suppliers and sources of financing, lobbying to place allies in peer positions, and even restructuring their boards to create networks favorable to their business goals. Jody abjured such tactics, but her adversaries did not.

Strategic networking can be difficult for emerging leaders because it absorbs a significant amount of the time and energy that managers usually devote to meeting their many operational demands. This is one reason why many managers drop their strategic networking precisely when they need it most: when their units are in trouble and only outside support can rescue them. The trick is not to hide in the operational network but to develop it into a more strategic one.

One manager we studied, for example, used lateral and functional contacts throughout his firm to resolve tensions with his boss that resulted from substantial differences in style and strategic approaches between the two. Tied down in operational chores at a distant location, the manager had lost contact with headquarters. He resolved the situation by simultaneously obliging his direct reports to take on more of the local management effort and sending messages through his network that would help bring him back into the loop with the boss.

Operational, personal, and strategic networks are not mutually exclusive. One manager we studied used his personal passion, hunting, to meet people from professions as diverse as stonemasonry and household moving. Almost none of these hunting friends had anything to do with his work in the consumer electronics industry, yet they all had to deal with one of his own daily concerns: customer relations. Hearing about their problems and techniques allowed him to view his own from a different perspective and helped him define principles that he could test in his work. Ultimately, what began as a personal network of hunting partners became operationally and strategically valuable to this manager. The key was his ability to build inside-outside links for maximum leverage. But we've seen others who avoided networking, or failed at it, because they let interpersonal chemistry, not strategic needs, determine which relationships they cultivated.

Just Do It

The word "work" is part of networking, and it is not easy work, because it involves reaching outside the borders of a manager's comfort zone. How, then, can managers lessen the pain and increase the gain? The trick is to leverage the elements from each domain of networking into the others—to seek out personal contacts who can be objective, strategic counselors, for example, or to transform colleagues in adjacent functions into a constituency. Above all, many managers will need to change their attitudes about the legitimacy and necessity of networking.

MIND YOUR MIND-SET

In our ongoing discussions with managers learning to improve their networking skills, we often hear, "That's all well and good, but I already have a day job." Others, like Jody, consider working through networks a way to rely on "whom you know" rather than "what you know"—a hypocritical, even unethical way to get things done. Whatever the reason, when aspiring leaders do not believe that networking is one of the most important requirements of their new jobs, they will not allocate enough time and effort to see it pay off.

The best solution we've seen to this trap is a good role model. Many times, what appears to be unpalatable or unproductive behavior takes on a new light when a person you respect does it well and ethically. For example, Gabriel Chenard, general manager for Europe of a group of consumer product brands, learned from the previous general manager how to take advantage of branch visits to solidify his relationships with employees and customers. Every flight and car trip became a venue for catching up and building relationships with the people who were accompanying him. Watching how much his boss got done on what would otherwise be downtime, Gabriel adopted the practice as a crucial part of his own management style. Networking effectively and ethically, like any other tacit skill, is a matter of judgment and intuition. We learn by observing and getting feedback from those for whom it's second nature.

WORK FROM THE OUTSIDE IN

One of the most daunting aspects of strategic networking is that there often seems to be no natural "excuse" for making contact with a more senior person outside one's function or business unit. It's difficult to build a relationship with anyone, let alone a senior executive, without a reason for interacting, like a common task or a shared purpose.

Some successful managers find common ground from the outside in—by, for instance, transposing a personal interest into the strategic domain. Linda Henderson is a good example. An investment banker responsible for a group of media industry clients, she always wondered how to connect to some of her senior colleagues who served other industries. She resolved to make time for an extracurricular passion—the theater—in a way that would enhance her business development activities. Four times a year, her secretary booked a buffet dinner at a downtown hotel and reserved a block of theater tickets. Key clients were invited. Through these events, Linda not only developed her own business but also learned about her clients' companies in a way that generated ideas for other parts of her firm, thus enabling her to engage with colleagues.

Other managers build outside-inside connections by using their functional interests or expertise. For example, communities of practice exist (or can easily be created on the Internet) in almost every area of business from brand management to Six Sigma to global strategy.

Savvy managers reach out to kindred spirits outside their organizations to contribute and multiply their knowledge; the information they glean, in more cases than not, becomes the "hook" for making internal connections.

RE-ALLOCATE YOUR TIME

If an aspiring leader has not yet mastered the art of delegation, he or she will find many reasons not to spend time networking. Participating in formal and informal meetings with people in other units takes time away from functional responsibilities and internal team affairs. Between the obvious payoff of a task accomplished and the ambiguous, often delayed rewards of networking, naive managers repeatedly choose the former. The less they practice networking, the less efficient at it they become, and the vicious cycle continues.

Henrik, the production manager and board member we described earlier, for example, did what he needed to do in order to prepare for board meetings but did not associate with fellow board members outside those formal events. As a result, he was frequently surprised when other board members raised issues at the heart of his role. In contrast, effective business leaders spend a lot of time every day gathering the information they need to meet their goals, relying on informal discussions with a lot of people who are not necessarily in charge of an issue or task. They network in order to obtain information continually, not just at formal meetings.

ASK AND YOU SHALL RECEIVE

Many managers equate having a good network with having a large database of contacts, or attending high-profile professional conferences and events. In fact, we've seen people kick off a networking initiative by improving their record keeping or adopting a network management tool. But they falter at the next step—picking up the phone. Instead, they wait until they need something *badly*. The best networkers do exactly the opposite: They take every opportunity to give to, and receive from, the network, whether they need help or not.

A network lives and thrives only when it is used. A good way to begin is to make a simple request or take the initiative to connect two people who would benefit from meeting each other. Doing something—anything—gets the ball rolling and builds confidence that one does, in fact, have something to contribute.

STICK TO IT

It takes a while to reap the benefits of networking. We have seen many managers resolve to put networking at the top of their agendas, only to be derailed by the first crisis that comes along. One example is Harris Roberts, a regulatory affairs expert who realized he needed a broader network to achieve his goal of becoming a business unit manager. To force himself into what felt like an "unnatural act," Harris volunteered to be the liaison for his business school cohort's alumni network. But six months later, when a major new-drug approval process overwhelmed his calendar, Harris dropped all outside activities. Two years later, he found himself out of touch and still a functional manager. He failed to recognize that by not taking the time to attend industry conferences or compare notes with his peers, he was missing out on the strategic perspective and information that would make him a more attractive candidate for promotion.

Building a leadership network is less a matter of skill than of will. When first efforts do not bring quick rewards, some may simply conclude that networking isn't among their talents. But networking is not a talent; nor does it require a gregarious, extroverted personality. It is a skill, one that takes practice. We have seen over and over again that people who work at networking can learn not only how to do it well but also how to enjoy it. And they tend to be more successful in their careers than those who fail to leverage external ties or insist on defining their jobs narrowly.

Making a successful leadership transition requires a shift from the confines of a clearly defined operational network. Aspiring leaders must learn to build and use strategic networks that cross organizational and functional boundaries, and then link them up in novel and innovative ways. It is a challenge to make the leap from a lifetime of functional contributions and hands-on control to the ambiguous process of building and working through networks. Leaders must find new ways of defining themselves and develop new relationships to anchor and feed their emerging personas. They must also accept that networking is one of the most important requirements of their new leadership roles and continue to allocate enough time and effort to see it pay off.

From Functional Manager to Business Leader: How Companies Can Help

EXECUTIVES WHO OVERSEE management development know how to spot critical inflection points: the moments when highly successful people must change their perspective on what is important and, accordingly, how they spend their time. Many organizations still promote people on the basis of their performance in roles whose requirements differ dramatically from those of leadership roles. And many new leaders feel that they are going it alone, without coaching or guidance. By being sensitive to the fact that most strong technical or functional managers lack the capabilities required to build strategic networks that advance their personal and professional goals, human resources and learning professionals can take steps to help in this important area.

For example, Genesis Park, an innovative in-house leadership development program at Pricewaterhouse-Coopers, focuses explicitly on building networks. The five-month program, during which participants are released from their client responsibilities, includes business case development, strategic projects, team building, change management projects, and in-depth discussions with business leaders from inside and outside the company. The young leaders who participate end up with a strong internal-external nexus of ties to support them as their careers evolve.

Companies that recognize the importance of leadership networking can also do a lot to help people overcome their innate discomfort by creating natural ways for them to extend their networks. When Nissan CEO Carlos Ghosn sought to break down crippling internal barriers at the company, he created cross-functional teams of middle managers from diverse units and charged them with proposing solutions to problems ranging from supply costs to product design. Nissan subsequently institutionalized the teams, not just as a way to solve problems but also to encourage lateral networks. Rather than avoid the extra work, aspiring leaders ask for these assignments.

Most professional development is based on the notion that successful people acquire new role-appropriate skills as they move up the hierarchy. But making the transition from manager to leader requires subtraction as well as addition: To make room for new competencies, managers must rely less on their older, well-honed skills. To do so, they must change their perspective on how to add value and what to contribute. Eventually, they must also transform how they think and who they are. Companies that help their top talent reinvent themselves will better prepare them for a successful leadership transition.

Originally published in January 2007
Reprint R0701C; HBR OnPoint 1727

When a New Manager Takes Charge

JOHN J. GABARRO

Executive Summary

WHEN SOME MANAGERS take over a new job, they hit the ground running. They learn the ropes, get along with their bosses and subordinates, gain credibility, and ultimately master the situation. Others, however, don't do so well. What accounts for the difference?

In this article, first published in 1985, Harvard Business School professor John J. Gabarro relates the findings of two sets of field studies he conducted, covering 14 management successions. The first set was a three-year study of four newly assigned division presidents; the second consisted of ten historical case studies. The project comprised American and European organizations with sales varying from $1.2 million to $3 billion. It included turnarounds, normal situations, failures, and triumphs.

According to the author, the taking-charge process follows five predictable stages: taking hold, immersion, reshaping, consolidation, and refinement. These phases are characterized by a series of alternating periods of intense learning (immersion and refinement) and action (taking hold, reshaping, and consolidation). The study's results put to rest the myth of the all-purpose general manager who can be dropped into any situation and emerge triumphant. Understanding a situation and effecting change do not occur overnight, says Gabarro, and human variables such as managerial styles and effective working relationships make a difference.

THE SUBSIDIARY WAS in serious trouble, so top management hired a young vice president of marketing with an enviable track record in another industry and gave him carte blanche. He reorganized the marketing function using a brand management concept, restructured the sales division, and devised new marketing strategies. Margins continued to erode, however, and after nine months he lost his job.

In another company, top management also hired a manager from a different industry to turn around a subsidiary's heavy losses and gave him considerable latitude. He too formulated an entirely new marketing strategy along brand lines. Within a year's time, margins improved, and within three years the subsidiary was very profitable and sales had doubled.

On the surface, these two situations are strikingly similar. Both executives were in their middle thirties, and neither had experience in his new industry. The two men implemented major changes that were remarkably alike. Furthermore, both worked for difficult bosses. Yet one succeeded and the other failed. What factors account for the different outcomes?

To answer this question, we need to look deeper and explore the contexts the two managers faced, their backgrounds, and the taking-charge process itself.

Although only dramatic examples make headlines, a recent study shows that by the time general managers reach their late forties, they have already taken charge of three to nine management posts.[1] Despite the frequency, however, and because situations are unique and managers so different, it is difficult to generalize about the taking-charge process.

Having studied 14 management successions, though, I have found issues common to all and factors that not only affect them but also influence how successful a new person is likely to be. (See the exhibit "The Managers Taking Charge," which details the research process.)

In using the term *taking charge,* I am referring to the process of learning and taking action that a manager goes through until he (or she) has mastered a new assignment in sufficient depth to be running the organization as well as resources and constraints allow.

The taking-charge process occurs in several predictable stages, each of which has its own tasks, problems, and dilemmas. My study's findings also put to rest the myth of the all-purpose general manager who can be dropped into any situation and triumph. To the contrary, my observations indicate that managers' experiences have a profound and inescapable influence on how they take charge, what areas they focus on, and how successful they are likely to be in mastering the new situation.

The New Manager Arrives

When I looked at the taking-charge process for a period of time, two patterns stood out. First, the process can be long. In the cases studied, for senior U.S. managers, it

The Managers Taking Charge

This article is based on a research project that consisted of two sets of field studies totaling 14 management successions. The first set was a longitudinal study of four newly assigned division presidents whom I studied over a three-year period as they went about the process of taking charge. The second set consisted of ten historical case studies of management successions, which were used to expand on and verify the longitudinal studies' results. The 14 cases were chosen to get a range of different kinds of management successions involving both functional and general managers. The successions included American and European organizations varying in sales from $1.2 million to $3 billion. The sample included turnarounds and normal situations and successions that failed as well as those that succeeded.

I studied the longitudinal cases using company documents, on-site observation, and field interviews with the new presidents and their subordinates at the end of three, six, 12, 15, 18, 24, 27, 30, and 36 months. For the historical studies, field interviews were conducted and company documents were used.

SUMMARY DESCRIPTION OF MANAGERS STUDIED

Unit's business	Unit revenues*	Manager's job	Predecessor as superior	Turnaround situation	Industry-specific experience	Insider (I) or outsider (O) to organization	Location	Succession success (S) or failure (F)†
Longitudinal case studies								
Industrial and office products division	$260 million	Division president	yes	no	yes	I	U.S.	S
Machine tool division	$175 million	Division president	no	yes	no	O	U.S.	S

business	revenues*	job	as superior	situation	industry-specific experience	Insider (I) or outsider (O) to organization	Location	Succession success (S) or failure (F)†
Consumer products division	$70 million	Division president	no	yes	no	O	U.S.	S
Construction products division	$55 million	Division president	yes	no	no	O	U.S.	S
				Historical case studies				
Cable television subsidiary	$1.2 million	General manager	no	no	no	O	U.S.	F
Wholesale food distributor	$21 million	Functional head	no	yes	no	O	U.S.	F
District sales organization (communications)	$30 million	Functional head	no	no	yes	I	U.S.	S
Beverage manufacturer	$90 million	General manager	no	yes	no	O	Netherlands	S
Plastic and metal products	$100 million	General manager	yes	no	yes	I	UK	F
Beverage manufacturer	$110 million	Functional head	yes	no	no	O	Italy	F
Synthetic fibers	$200 million	Functional head	yes	yes	yes	I	UK	S
Computer and technical products	$780 million	General manager	no	no	yes	I	Switzerland	S
Industrial and consumer products	$3 billion	General manager	no	yes	yes	I	UK	S
Public education	Not available	Functional manager	no	yes	yes	I	U.S	S

* Unit revenues expressed in 1982 U.S. dollars.

† A succession was considered a failure if the new manager was fired within the first 36 months because of his inability to meet top management's expectations of performance.

took from two to two and a half years; some European and UK senior managers took even longer. Second, the taking-charge process does not involve steadily more learning or action. Rather, it is a series of alternating phases of intense learning and intense action. Also, the nature of both the managers' learning and actions changes over time.

With few exceptions, most new managers' organizational changes tended to cluster in three bursts of activity. Exhibit I shows these periods quite clearly. Exhibit II illustrates that the same bursts occur regardless of the type of succession. The data presented in Exhibits I, II, III, and IV are for completed successions only, in other words, those in which the new manager lasted in the job for two and a half years or longer. As such, the exhibits do not include data from three of the failed successions. The organizational activity measure is a composite of both structural and personnel changes managers made.

What accounts for this pervasive pattern? Why were the major changes made almost invariably in three waves of action? My observations suggest that the

Exhibit I

Average Number of Organizational Changes per Three-Month Period Following Succession

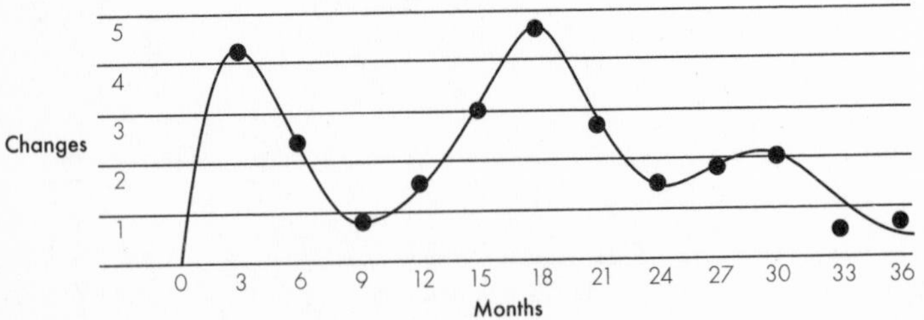

underlying patterns of learning and action account for these periods of intense change. They are natural consequences of how new managers learn and act as they try to master strange situations. More specifically, the data suggest that the taking-charge process occurs in five predictable stages: taking hold, immersion, reshaping, consolidation, and refinement. The length of time the executives I studied spent in each stage varied. Some spent as long as 11 months and others as little as four in the same stage. Thus, time doesn't define a stage; rather, the

---

Exhibit II

Average Number of Organizational Changes per Six-Month Period Following Succession, Categorized

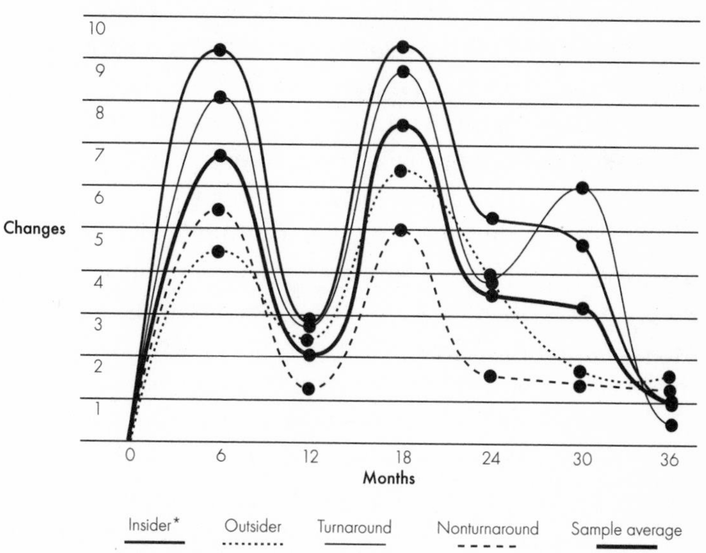

*Insider successions are those in which the new manager had five or more years' experience in the new organization's industry.

nature of learning and the action that characterizes it does. Let's look at each stage more carefully.

TAKING HOLD

The first stage, taking hold, typically lasts from three to six months and often sets the tone, if not the direction, for the rest of the taking-charge process. (Exhibit III shows the percentages of personnel and structural changes by six-month periods, which the managers made during their successions.) Taking hold is a period of intense action and learning. If the new assignment is a big promotion or change, the newcomer may at times feel overwhelmed. A new division president commented:

"You're on the edge of your seat all the time. It feels like you have no knowledge base whatsoever. You have to learn the product, the people, and the problems. You're trying like hell to learn about the organization and the people awfully fast, and that's the trickiest thing. At first you're afraid to do anything for fear of upsetting the apple cart. The problem is you have to keep the business running while you're learning about it."

During this period, a manager is grappling with the nature of the new situation, trying to understand the tasks and problems and assessing the organization and its requirements. Managers orient themselves, evaluate the situation, and develop a cognitive map. For example, one division president who was an industry outsider described his learning task as so large that even locking himself up for four days to review strategic, financial, marketing, and industry reports barely made a dent. Early in this stage, he also reported that it took him several hours to go through the morning mail, not only because the issues were new to him but also because the industry had its own technical jargon and nomenclature.

Another manager in a similar situation voiced his exasperation by saying resignedly, "There aren't enough hours in the day." (All of the managers in the study happened to be men. I have every reason to believe that female managers would go through the same stages.)

Evaluation and orientation in the taking-hold stage are important even for insiders who already know of the organization and the product. A division president with

---

Exhibit III
Personnel and Structural Changes Made (by six-month periods)

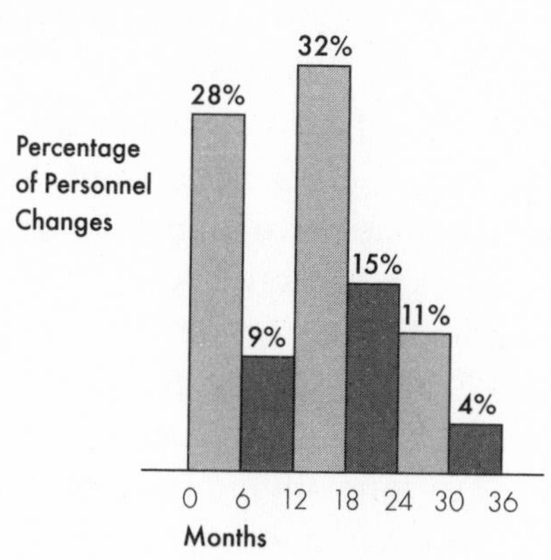

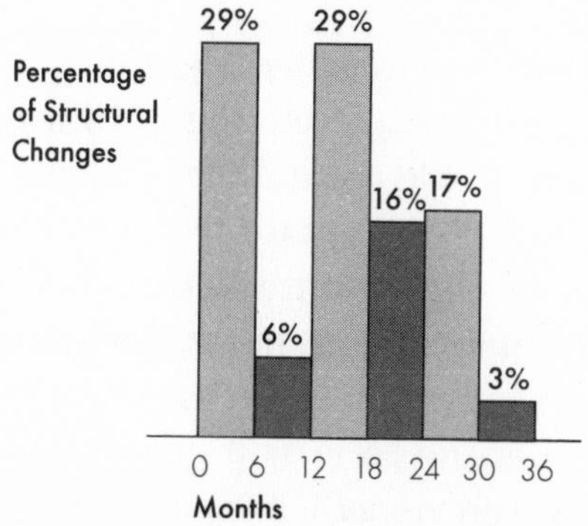

more than 25 years in his organization spent the first three months in his new job testing his assumptions about key people and the division's problems. He came to several conclusions, one of which was that a senior vice president in his group was in over his head. The division president based his assessment on a number of meetings with the senior vice president, his subordinates' opinions, his plan for the previous five years, complaints about cliques in his area, problems with division functions, and the senior VP's insensitive treatment of two of the company's major overseas distributors. The last item was particularly troublesome because it made the new president doubt the man's judgment. Questioning previous perceptions and beliefs characterized most insider successions during this stage.

Actions taken during the taking-hold stage tend to be corrective. Based on their experience and what they have learned about the new situation, managers fix what problems they can. Obviously, corrective actions vary—some are short-term interventions, others take longer. For instance, in one case, although it took nearly five months before the new manager had developed a strategy for turning around the division, because of his experience, within a month he knew that the division needed both a cost system and a product-line reduction immediately.

A group CEO approached this stage quite differently, however. Having been promoted from within and having himself previously turned around the business's manufacturing operation, he did not make significant short-term corrections his first priority. Rather, focusing on product strategy and planning, he established committees and teams to address these areas. Although his actions did not have the same fix-it quality of the other turnaround, they were nonetheless corrective in that they dealt with areas the new CEO considered critical to the group's success.

The magnitude of corrective action also varies. In his third month in office, a division president with 25 years of experience in the company reorganized his new area. In contrast, the division presidents who were outsiders did not implement comparable changes until their second year in office, when they were well beyond the taking-hold stage.

IMMERSION

Compared with the taking-hold stage, the immersion period is quiet. Exhibit III shows a dramatic decrease in changes after the first six months: Only 6% of organizational and 9% of personnel changes occurred during the second six months, a time period that generally coincided with the beginning of the immersion phase. A lull between bursts of activity, immersion is a very significant time, however, during which executives acquire greater understanding of their new situations. In the U.S. cases I studied, this stage lasted four to 11 months.

During immersion, new managers run the organization in a more informed fashion and steep themselves in a less hectic, finer-grained learning process than was possible when they were taking hold. Consequently, by the end of this stage, they have developed a new concept or at least have greatly revised their ideas of what they need to do.

More focused learning happens during this period because managers immerse themselves in running the organization, and they learn from the interactions and conflicts they deal with day to day. As their experience base grows, they can see patterns they didn't see before. In one case, for example, even though the new division manager made several momentous changes—reorganizing manufacturing by product lines and implementing better control, scheduling, and cost systems—during the taking-hold stage, manufacturing cost problems persisted. During the immersion stage, he was able to see that many of these had their roots in the product's design and, ultimately, in how the division's engineering group was structured. It took, however, six to eight months of exploration before this underlying cause became clear.

Even when changes made in the taking-hold stage work, the immersion period still offers opportunities for further learning. New problems that had been masked or overshadowed by larger problems emerge. For example, after a division president had reorganized his division from a functional to a geographic structure, with a domestic-international split, a new set of problems surfaced during the immersion period that neither he nor his management team had foreseen. The earlier reorganization significantly increased the responsiveness, productivity, and coordination between functions in the United States and abroad, but as these areas improved, the U.S. sales force's organization and its distribution channels showed weaknesses. The old structure's cross-functional problems had hidden these weaknesses.

During immersion, new managers also question whether they have the right people in place. Obvious questions about competence arose in the taking-hold stage, but now they were easier to discern. Similarly, in more than half the cases studied, the newcomers explored uncertainties they had about staff members and discussed them with others.

The analysis, probes, discussions, and, in some cases, agony of the immersion stage result in new managers' arriving at a better understanding of the more basic dynamics of the organization, people, and the industry. The concept that emerges from this stage (whether new or refined) is not necessarily radical. In six of the 14 cases, however, the revised concept had implications for radical changes in either strategy or organization or both. In most of the cases, it also resulted in a sharper plan of action for improving the situation further.

RESHAPING

During the third stage, reshaping, the second important—and in most cases the largest—burst of activity takes place. Learning continues but in a more diminished and routine fashion. In the reshaping period, new managers direct their attention toward reconfiguring one or more aspects of the organization to implement the concept they developed or made final during the immersion stage.

The reshaping stage, like the taking-hold period, involves a great deal of organizational change. Exhibit III shows that more than 32% of the personnel changes and 29% of the structural changes were made during the third six-month period. Again I should caution that the stages did not neatly apportion themselves out into six-month periods. Nonetheless, after 13 to 18 months, most managers studied had reached the reshaping stage, where they were eager to act on the learning and exploration they had experienced in the immersion period. Indeed, immersion activities usually pave the way for reshaping-stage changes.

Immersion is a transition, and by the end of it, new managers and often their key subordinates are impatient to get on with things. In one case, for example, a new division president had to fend off growing pressure from two of his vice presidents while he commissioned several task forces to focus on the areas of intended change. As he put it, "The task force reports will take us to the point where there will be no surprises and a lot of added insights. The nice part of this is that everyone will know what needs to be done, and they'll have ownership of the changes we decide to make. If the obvious answer is wrong, the reports will flush it out. In the meantime, I have to convince the guys down the hall that the added time this requires is worth it."

Reshaping-stage changes may involve altering processes as well as making major structural shifts. Two divisions studied went from product to functional structures.

As one would imagine, the reshaping stage is very busy, especially if it involves major changes. For example, when one manager was reorganizing both marketing and sales, he had to call two series of meetings (one with the affected managers and another with the district sales forces to explain the changes), work out details where positional changes and relocations were involved, and call on key customers and distributors. Thus, although management announced plans for the changes at the outset of this stage, their implementation took nearly eight weeks of sustained activity on the part of the new president, his new marketing VP, and his domestic sales manager. As one would expect, the learning in the reshaping stage consists mainly of feedback, for example, on the impact the sales reorganization had on key distributors and on orders.

Reshaping ends when new managers have implemented as much of their concept as circumstances allow. In practice, several factors (the most common is the unavailability of people for key positions) often prevent them from completing the job.

CONSOLIDATION

The third and final wave of action in the taking-charge process occurs during the fourth stage, consolidation. Throughout this period, much of new managers' learning and action focuses on consolidating and following through on the changes they made during reshaping. The process is evaluative; for example, new managers and their key subordinates judge the consequences of the actions they took in the reshaping burst of activity and take corrective measures.

Learning at this point involves two sets of issues, the first of which is identifying what the leftover follow-through implementation problems are and how to deal with them. For instance, during his reshaping stage, a new president had reorganized his division from a product to a functional structure. But he had deferred integrating one of the former product group's manufacturing departments into the divisional manufacturing function until several other changes had been completed. When most of the reorganization had been accomplished, he and his manufacturing vice president began to study how the product group could be integrated.

A second set of issues evolves from unanticipated problems resulting from changes made during the reshaping stage. Much of the consolidation period's extraordinary activity involves diagnosing and studying these problems, then correcting them.

Finally, during consolidation, new managers deal with those aspects of their concept that they could not implement before. In several situations, for instance, managers had to wait to find a person for an important position or to transfer one of the organization's managers who could not move earlier.

REFINEMENT

The refinement stage is a period of little organizational change. By this point, executives have taken charge, and their learning and actions tend to focus either on refining operations or on looking for opportunities in the marketplace, in technology, or in other areas. In one case, the manager looked at potential acquisitions; in another, the manager seriously considered divesting part of the business.

This stage marks the end of the taking-charge process. By this time managers can no longer be considered new. They no longer feel new, nor do their subordinates perceive or speak of them as new. Whatever the problems the executives now face, they do not result from newness. By now, they have either established credibility and a power base, or they have not. They have had enough time to shape their situations, and they will be judged by the results of their actions. If they are still uncomfortable, usually it is because of pressing business problems such as a recession or mounting interest rates rather than unfamiliarity with their jobs.

Refinement is a calm period. From this stage onward, managers' learning will be more incremental and routine. Important developments in the economy, the marketplace, or technology may destroy this calmness, but whatever additional learning and action such factors lead to, they do not result from newness. For better or worse, the manager has taken charge.

What Makes a Difference?

A number of factors shape how executives progress through these stages and how successfully they take charge. Important determinants include a new manager's experience, whether the business needs turning around, the person's managerial style and personal needs, his relationships with key people by the end of the first year, and whether the manager's management style conflicts with that of his boss. Let me describe each of these in more detail.

ROOTS THAT ENDURE

All other things being equal, managers' functional backgrounds, managerial experiences, and special competencies appear to determine how they take charge: what actions they take and how competently they implement them.

The extent to which managers' functional experience influences their actions is quite surprising. For 13 of the 14 new managers studied, their initial actions were in areas where they had had functional experience, and the most significant changes they made during the three years also were in the areas where they had experience (see Exhibit IV). This pattern is not surprising for functional managers. But emergence of the same pattern among the general managers reveals the extent to which experience influences actions and points of view.

Because Exhibit IV is a summary, it understates both the specificity and pervasiveness of how much the new managers' experience affected their actions. Exhibit V looks at ten managers' experience and actions in some detail.

Exhibit IV

Summary of How Managers' Functional Experience Affected Their Actions

		LONGITUDINAL STUDIES				HISTORICAL STUDIES									
		Division presidents				**Other general managers**					**Functional managers**				
		1	2	3	4	5	6	7	8	9	10	11	12	13	14
Actions taken	**Initial actions**														
	Initial activities were in area of prior functional experience.	X	X	X	X	X	X	X	X	X	X	X	NO	X	X
	First structural change affected area of prior functional experience.	X	X	X	X	X	NO	NA	X	X	X	NA	NO	X	NA
	Major action														
	Most significant change made in first three years affected area of prior functional experience.	X	X	X	X	X	X	X	X	X	X	X	NO	X	X
	Most significant structural change affected area of prior functional experience.	X	X	X	X	X	X	NA	X	X	X	NA	X	X	NA

X = yes
NO = no
NA = not available

If one thinks in terms of the five taking-charge stages, this pattern is not so surprising. Indeed, one could predict that any significant additional experience base managers gain as a result of taking charge of a new assignment will not be firm until after they have experienced the deeper learning of the immersion stage, acted on this knowledge in the reshaping stage, and learned from these actions in the consolidation stage.

INSIDERS VERSUS OUTSIDERS

New managers' experience in their organization's industry also affected significantly how they took charge and what problems they encountered. First, industry insiders (managers who have five or more years' experience in the new organization's industry) take hold much more quickly than do outsiders. Insiders begin with a larger wave of action and their actions tend to be more basic. For example, fully 33% of all of the structural changes industry insiders made occurred during their first six months. Second, the number of actions insiders take is greater not only in the taking-hold stage (in the study, on average, insiders' actions were twice as frequent) but throughout the entire taking-charge process. Moreover, whereas three of four of the managers who did not succeed in their jobs lacked industry experience, only four of ten successful managers lacked such experience (I defined a failed appointment as one in which the new manager was fired within three years of taking charge).

One case, in which a marketing manager with more than 15 years' experience in packaged goods and toiletries became marketing and sales director of a $110 million beverage division, illustrates an outsider's difficulties. On the surface, his background looked like a

Exhibit V
Comparison of Managers' Functional Experience and Actions Taken (historical studies)

Business, manager's title, and company sales ⟶	Cable television subsidiary General manager $1.2 million	Wholesale food distribution Vice president–marketing and sales $21 million
Prior assignment	Communications engineer (in another company)	Vice president-marketing and planning (in another company)
Functional experience	Engineering	Marketing and product management
Initial area of major involvement	Construction and engineering Planning	Product planning and reduction of sales force
Areas affected by first structural change	Engineering installation and construction	Creation of product manager's position and reorganization of product sales groups
Areas affected by major structural change	Same	Marketing (creation of product manager's responsibilities)
Areas affected by most significant changes of first three years	Reorganization of chief engineer's department affecting engineering, construction, and installation	Introduction of product management

District sales service organization District manager $30 million	Beverage manufacturer Division general manager $80 million	Plastic and metal products Group managing director $100 million
Sales service administrator (in same company)	Division general manager (in another company)	Division general manager (in same company)
Customer service	Marketing and market planning (also experience in two prior turnarounds as general manager)	Manufacturing and engineering
Sales service audit	Sales force and marketing	Manufacturing rationalization
(No structural changes made)	Sales force	(No structural changes made)
(No structural changes made)	Creation of marketing function and reorganization of sales force	(No structural changes made)
Sales service training	Revision of mission scope and revamping of marketing strategy affecting marketing and sales	Manufacturing rationalization

continued

Exhibit V (continued)
Comparison of Managers' Functional Experience and Actions Taken (historical studies)

Business, manager's title, and company sales ⟶	**Beverage manufacturer Director of marketing and sales $110 million**	**Synthetic fibers Director of manufacturing $300 million**
Prior assignment	Marketing and sales director (in another company)	Works manager (in same company)
Functional experience	Marketing	Manufacturing and engineering
Initial area of major involvement	Sales and sales procedures and information systems	Restructuring of manufacturing management
Areas affected by first structural change	Sales force	Manufacturing
Areas affected by major structural change	Sales and marketing	Same
Areas affected by most significant changes of first three years	Sales systems and procedures	Rationalization and restructuring of production operations

Computer and technical products Group vice president and general manager $780 million	Industrial and consumer Group CEO $3 billion	Public education Administrator
Group general marketing manager (in same company)	Group manufacturing director (in same company)	Administrator (in same system)
Marketing, sales operations, and engineering	Manufacturing management and production control (turnaround experience)	Educational administration (turnaround experience)
Marketing and sales operations	Product strategy and product planning, manufacturing operations, and production engineering	School discipline, athletics and activities, accreditation, and community involvement
Group staff functions (finance, controller, group support functions)	Manufacturing and production engineering	(Not applicable)
Sales operations and marketing	Manufacturing, product engineering, and product planning	(Not applicable)
Restructuring of sales operations	Manufacturing operations, production engineering, quality control, and product planning	Discipline, academic standards, student activities, and community involvement

good fit, but the new industry was different from traditional packaged goods in a number of important ways. The outsider's experience had served him well in product planning and changing systems during the taking-hold period and later in restructuring the sales force. It had not, however, prepared him for dealing with the sales force or his major distributors, both of which required a hands-on approach. By the end of the taking-hold stage, he was in serious trouble with both groups. By the end of his first year, his cool, professional, managerial style had alienated some key distributors so much that the division general manager had to intervene in several critical situations. These incidents undermined the new manager's ability to develop credibility with customers and subordinates.

TURNING THINGS AROUND

How unfavorable a new situation was also influenced the taking-charge process in the cases I studied. In turnarounds managers feel a great deal of pressure to act on problems quickly. One might expect that in a turnaround, because of the urgency of the situation, executives would have a shorter taking-hold stage, but neither the aggregated data nor the individual case data support this. If anything, the data suggest that the taking-hold wave actually lasts longer in a turnaround.

Although the action waves are of comparable duration, the activity in the reshaping and consolidation stages peaks earlier in the turnarounds by about three to six months, a pattern which no doubt reflects the urgency experienced in turnarounds.

None of these differences between normal successions and turnarounds that the data uncovered is surprising.

Others, which surfaced in manager interviews, are. For one thing, turnaround managers told me they knew they would have to redo later some of the changes they were making in the taking-hold stage.

In one case, the new general manager reported he knew from experience (this was his third turnaround) that it would take five to six months to design and implement a cost system that was sophisticated enough to provide all the information he needed on which products were losing money and why. He concluded that he simply did not have the time to do it perfectly and opted instead for a system that would give him, as quickly as possible, a better vision of the problems.

Managers don't make such suboptimal decisions gladly. When new managers and their subordinates had fewer problems to deal with (usually in the consolidation period), they would go back and improve the tourniquet systems and processes they had installed earlier.

Although the turnaround managers were under much greater pressure than their nonturnaround counterparts, they benefited from certain advantages. Generally speaking, their companies gave them much more latitude in taking action than the managers had in the normal successions. This was particularly true during the taking-hold stage. The two situations I described in the beginning of the article illustrate this well.

In the first case, after six weeks on the job, the new marketing vice president proposed a wholly new marketing strategy that top management rapidly approved. Such agreeableness is rare in nonturnaround successions. In the second case, the new manager's head office not only gave him a much greater degree of freedom than it usually gave its division general managers, but it also buffered him from corporate staff intervention for the first two years. After the manager completed the turnaround, top management told him he now had to play by the rules and conform more closely to corporate policies.

Generally, because of the urgency of the situations, the turnaround managers started with a larger power base than their counterparts and faced less rivalry from key subordinates who might have wanted their jobs. But several turnaround managers reported feeling their organizations were fearful and tense, which put additional pressure on them to settle things as quickly as possible.

THE NEW MANAGER'S STYLE

The 14 men I studied varied significantly in their styles, including how they spent their time—alone, in meetings, on tours—what kinds of meetings and interactions they preferred—one-to-one, recurrently scheduled or specially scheduled meetings, planned meetings versus ad hoc meetings—and their preferences for formality or informality.

Managerial style affects how people respond to an executive initially and influences the entire taking-charge process, including how the person makes decisions. The most dramatic example of this was one president who had a fairly hands-on approach to problems and needed control. Because he thought that the product organization prevented him from seeing problems at the functional level, he struggled throughout the immersion stage. Finally, he reorganized the division from a product to a functional structure. The implementation of this change was painful for the organization and required that several functional vice presidents split their time among three businesses, two of which were geographically separated, so that they had to travel every week. Nonetheless, the total succession went very well.

For this president, acting according to his style was a necessity. During the final debriefing in the study's fourth year, he told me that he believed he could not have turned the company around without restructuring it to fit his needs. His successor introduced a series of changes, which again made the organization more product oriented.

RELATIONSHIPS WITH KEY PEOPLE

Perhaps the single most salient difference between the successful and the failed transitions was the quality of the new manager's working relationships at the end of his first year. For example, at this point, three of four managers in the failed successions had poor working relationships with two or more of their key subordinates and with two or more peers, and all had poor working relationships with their superiors. In contrast, in the same time frame, only one of the new administrators in the successful transitions had a poor relationship with his boss and none had poor relationships with two or more people who reported directly to them.

Many reasons were given for these interpersonal problems, such as rivalry issues, disagreement about goals, different beliefs about what constituted effective performance, and conflicts in management style. The underlying common problem, however, was the new managers' failure to develop a set of shared expectations with their key subordinates or their bosses. Without common understanding, each side in the relationships inevitably stopped trusting the other.

The studies showed that developing effective working relationships was a critical task in the taking-hold and immersion stages. If managers didn't explore important differences in the very beginning of their successions, further problems would crop up. Managers in the successful transitions usually confronted problems by the end of the immersion stage and resolved them either by attaining agreement or by parting company.

CONFLICTS IN MANAGEMENT STYLE

Surprisingly, many of the new managers studied (six of 14) described a conflict in styles with their bosses as being a major problem in taking charge. Although conflicts and differences in styles also existed in relationships with subordinates, I am highlighting the problem between new managers and their bosses because this type of discord characterized all but one of the failed successions.

The conflicts always involved control and delegation. In one case, for example, a new general manager five months into the job was exasperated because his boss wouldn't stop a capital request that the manager's predecessor had submitted. The boss had asked his technical and financial staffs to review the situation and was waiting for their report before acting. This manager also reported difficulty in getting quick answers from his boss about operational questions. The manager thought his boss delegated too much and wasn't on top of details.

In contrast, another new executive felt he couldn't get his boss off his back. The situation finally exploded at the end of the first year when his boss gave him a poor performance evaluation for not being involved enough in details and for delegating too much to his subordinates.

In both these cases, the conflicts arose partly because managers hadn't clarified expectations with their bosses but mainly because of less rational factors, including profound beliefs about what is good management. Namely, a good executive sets goals clearly and delegates responsibility to subordinates without interfering, while a good manager gets involved in details and is action oriented and decisive.

How can new managers deal with differences in style? In the cases studied, the new managers had to take the initiative to work out differences and make the accommodations needed for working effectively with their bosses. In the first case, for example, the new manager stopped pressing his boss about the capital project; instead he worked with the two staff groups who were conducting the review. The second manager defined his performance targets specifically with his boss, so the boss could delegate to him more comfortably.

In the three successful transitions marked by sharp style conflicts, the managers employed similar means to deal with them.

HOW STACKED IS THE DECK?

As we can see, many variables influence how well managers take charge. Critical factors range from managers' experience to how effectively they deal with key subordinates and their bosses. Although some are more critical than others, no one factor dominates. Evaluated together, however, they can indicate how much difficulty a new manager will face. Let me illustrate this by returning to the two vignettes that began this article. On the surface they looked so similar, but they turned out so differently.

In the first case, in which the new marketing vice president lasted only nine months, his lack of industry experience hurt him considerably, especially since both his immediate boss and the division's parent management also lacked industry experience. His boss's failure to clarify his expectations about performance and a major conflict in management style between the two men further exacerbated the situation. Finally, a poor working relationship with an important peer, who sought to undermine the new manager, complicated his difficulties.

If the deck is stacked, as it was in this case, unless the new manager or his boss is insightful enough to defuse, compensate for, or in some other way minimize problems, the succession is doomed. In the other case, although the parameters were the same, the dynamics among the players were quite different, so that the second new manager prospered where the other failed.

Managing the New Manager

This study's findings offer several implications that, taken together, challenge a number of assumptions and current practices. First, we can see clearly that understanding a situation and having an impact on it do not occur overnight. Fast-track developmental assignments do not, in the end, benefit the individual, the new unit, or the organization.

Second, the all-purpose general manager who can parachute into any situation and succeed is a myth. Experience and special competencies do matter.

Finally, human variables such as managerial styles make a difference, not only to the organization's climate but also to the business decisions a new manager makes and to how he implements them.

Other soft factors, such as potential conflicts in managerial styles and a newcomer's ability to develop effective working relationships, also seriously affect outcomes. These are, however, subjective factors that often fall into the nondiscussable category that senior management seldom considers when it plans successions. Only the savviest planners factor them in and give them the weight they deserve.

Let me be more specific about the findings' implications for both managers who are taking charge and organizations that must be concerned with succession planning and career development.

WHEN YOU ARE TAKING CHARGE

For a manager in the middle of taking charge, this article may be a mixed blessing. On the one hand, it may be a relief to know that the process occurs in stages that consist of predictable learning and action tasks (see the exhibit "Taking Charge: Tasks and Dilemmas" for a summary). On the other, to realize that there may still be considerable learning and action to accomplish after the first three to six months on the job can be a bit dismaying.

The other potentially unsettling implication is that in each of these stages the manager is on a tightrope. For example, if the taking-hold stage is a bit of a honeymoon, it is also a period in which new managers must establish their credibility. If they act too slowly, they risk losing the honeymoon period's advantages as well as valuable time, and they can appear indecisive. But if new executives act too quickly, they risk making poor decisions because of inadequate knowledge, or they take actions that preclude options they may later wish they had.

Managers who are industry outsiders are on particularly slippery ground. In the absence of good advice or

Taking Charge: Tasks and Dilemmas

I Taking hold: orientation and evaluation, corrective actions	Tasks	Develop an understanding of the new situation
		Take corrective actions
		Develop initial set of priorities and "map" of the situation
		Develop initial set of expectations with key subordinates
		Establish the basis for effective working relationships
	Dilemma	How quickly to act on apparent problems?
		Act too quickly—risks:
		Make a poor decision because of lack of adequate information or knowledge
		Take actions that constrain subsequent decisions that cannot be anticipated yet
		Act too slowly—risks:
		Lose advantages of the "honeymoon" period
		Lose credibility because of apparent indecisiveness
		Lose valuable time

II Immersion: **fine-grained, exploratory learning and managing the business**	Tasks	Develop a deeper, finer-grained understanding of the new situation and the people
		Assess consequences of taking-hold period actions
		Reassess priorities
		Settle questions and problems concerning key personnel
		Reconfigure "map" of the situation; fill out or revise the concept
		Prepare for reshaping actions
III Reshaping: **acting on the revised concept**	Tasks	Reconfigure organization based on finer-grained understanding
		Deal with underlying causes of residual problems
		Be open to unanticipated problems that emerge as a result of second-wave changes
IV Consolidation: **evaluative learning, follow-through, and corrective action**	Tasks	Follow through on reshaping actions
		Deal with unanticipated problems of reshaping stage
		Remain open to new developments
V Refinement: **refining operations, looking for new opportunities**		

data, they may be better off deferring major changes until they have learned more in the immersion stage. The small first waves of action and large second waves in the outsider successions I studied probably reflect an intuitive recognition of this dilemma.

Finally, interpersonal factors emerge in one fashion or another. If, for example, newcomers find themselves in a managerial style conflict, they should not think it's bizarre; it occurred in almost half the situations I studied.

In general, a comparison of failed and effective transitions indicates that front-end work is crucial, especially in working out parameters and expectations with bosses. In the successful successions, the new managers made their mandates as specific and explicit as possible. They also made a point of keeping their superiors informed, for example, discussing with them changes they were proposing in detail—particularly during the early taking-charge stages. In contrast, the managers who failed carried vague mandates.

The successful managers were also more aware of their limitations in experience or skills and compensated for them either with selective learning or by drawing on their colleagues' abilities.

SUCCESSION PLANNING AND CAREER DEVELOPMENT

As the preceding discussion suggests, top management can take a number of steps to help minimize new administrators' problems. The most obvious of these is making the new person's charter explicit. If this is not possible (because top management doesn't understand the unit's business or the industry is in a period of turmoil), the new manager should know it. For example, in the opening vignette in which the new manager failed after nine months, headquarters hadn't told him that the most urgent priority was to reverse a decline in the newly acquired subsidiary's margins. The innocent new vice president started off buying market share, which inevitably eroded further the margins in the short term.

There are other things companies can do to facilitate the taking-charge process. General Electric, for example, runs assimilation meetings to accelerate working out expectations between new managers and their key subordinates. Conducted by the human resource staff, these meetings give new managers and those who report directly to them the opportunity to talk about expectations and other concerns early in a new manager's tenure. Top management can also anticipate the potential problems new managers who lack relevant experience face, particularly during the taking-charge stages, and lessen them by providing adequate—subordinate or corporate—backup support.

An important implication of this research for succession planning is that taking charge (defined in terms of impact and learning) takes time. Companies that make brief assignments at upper and middle levels will get quick fixes. If assignments are too short for a new manager to go beyond the taking-hold stage, the new manager will deal only with those problems that he or she knows how to fix. That may be enough if a manager's experience base is broad and deep, but when short-term assignments become company policy, both individual units and the organization as a whole suffer eventually. Taken to its extreme, such a policy feeds the obsession with short-term results that many observers have criticized.[2]

Short-term assignments also make little sense from a career development point of view. In most brief assignments, managers can't progress beyond the immersion stage. Yet the payoffs for the organization in substantive change and for the individual in important residual learning and added experience don't come until later. Significant new learning begins in the immersion stage when the outsider is familiar enough to probe underlying issues and subtle cause-and-effect relationships. Managers cannot test this new learning, though, until they act in the reshaping stage, evaluate their actions, and learn more in the consolidation and refinement stages.

The importance of experience also has several implications for succession planning and career development. All other factors being equal, an insider with industry-specific or other relevant experience is more likely to take charge with fewer difficulties than an outsider without industry-specific experience. Three of the four managers who failed were industry outsiders in well-run U.S. and European companies.

The importance of experience, which the study highlighted, also challenges the concept of the professional manager. Although turnaround specialists can succeed in a variety of situations, they are the exception, not the rule; in fact, they are themselves specialists of a kind.

I am not arguing that general management skills don't exist or that people can't transfer them into new settings. I am pointing out that lack of relevant industry or functional experience will make the taking-charge process more difficult, and companies should consider this when planning successions.

When choosing successors to managerial posts, top management has to make some difficult trade-offs in terms of what is good for the person, the unit, and the organization. If one of the organization's objectives is to develop a well-trained pool of managerial talent, then the head office should put executives in assignments that stretch them by broadening their experience. This will inevitably mean putting people with less than optimal experience in charge of units whose performance may suffer, at least in the short term. The question is whether the benefits to the person and to the larger organization are worth the costs. Also, because managers, like all human beings, learn from the feedback of bad as well as good experiences (some may argue they learn more from the ones that turn out badly), top management has to judge how long to keep executives in situations where they are having problems.

On the other hand, if management always assigns people with strong relevant experience, it forfeits giving executives broadening experiences, which become increasingly important at middle and upper levels. The guideline should be to provide developmental assignments that are not totally out of line with a manager's experience and that last long enough to produce important lessons.

Notes

1. John P. Kotter, *The General Managers* (Free Press, 1982).
2. Robert H. Hayes and William J. Abernathy, "Managing Our Way to Economic Decline," HBR July–August 1980.

Originally published in January 2007
Reprint R0701K

Leading Change

Why Transformation Efforts Fail

JOHN P. KOTTER

Executive Summary

BUSINESSES HOPING to survive over the long term will have to remake themselves into better competitors at least once along the way. These efforts have gone under many banners: total quality management, reengineering, rightsizing, restructuring, cultural change, and turnarounds, to name a few. In almost every case, the goal has been to cope with a new, more challenging market by changing the way business is conducted. A few of these endeavors have been very successful. A few have been utter failures. Most fall somewhere in between, with a distinct tilt toward the lower end of the scale.

John P. Kotter is renowned for his work on leading organizational change. In 1995, when this article was first published, he had just completed a ten-year study of more than 100 companies that attempted such a transformation. Here he shares the results of his observations, outlining the eight largest errors that can doom these efforts and explaining the general lessons that encourage success.

Unsuccessful transitions almost always founder during at least one of the following phases: generating a sense of urgency, establishing a powerful guiding coalition, developing a vision, communicating the vision clearly and often, removing obstacles, planning for and creating short-term wins, avoiding premature declarations of victory, and embedding changes in the corporate culture.

Realizing that change usually takes a long time, says Kotter, can improve the chances of success.

OVER THE PAST DECADE, I have watched more than 100 companies try to remake themselves into significantly better competitors. They have included large organizations (Ford) and small ones (Landmark Communications), companies based in the United States (General Motors) and elsewhere (British Airways), corporations that were on their knees (Eastern Airlines), and companies that were earning good money (Bristol-Myers Squibb). These efforts have gone under many banners: total quality management, reengineering, rightsizing, restructuring, cultural change, and turnaround. But, in almost every case, the basic goal has been the same: to make fundamental changes in how business is conducted in order to help cope with a new, more challenging market environment.

A few of these corporate change efforts have been very successful. A few have been utter failures. Most fall somewhere in between, with a distinct tilt toward the lower end of the scale. The lessons that can be drawn are interesting and will probably be relevant to even more organizations in the increasingly competitive business environment of the coming decade.

The most general lesson to be learned from the more successful cases is that the change process goes through a series of phases that, in total, usually require a considerable length of time. Skipping steps creates only the illusion of speed and never produces a satisfying result. A second very general lesson is that critical mistakes in any of the phases can have a devastating impact, slowing momentum and negating hard-won gains. Perhaps because we have relatively little experience in renewing organizations, even very capable people often make at least one big error.

Error 1: Not Establishing a Great Enough Sense of Urgency

Most successful change efforts begin when some individuals or some groups start to look hard at a company's competitive situation, market position, technological trends, and financial performance. They focus on the potential revenue drop when an important patent expires, the five-year trend in declining margins in a core business, or an emerging market that everyone seems to be ignoring. They then find ways to communicate this information broadly and dramatically, especially with respect to crises, potential crises, or great opportunities that are very timely. This first step is essential because just getting a transformation program started requires the aggressive cooperation of many individuals. Without motivation, people won't help, and the effort goes nowhere.

Compared with other steps in the change process, phase one can sound easy. It is not. Well over 50% of the companies I have watched fail in this first phase. What are the reasons for that failure? Sometimes executives underestimate how hard it can be to drive people out of their comfort zones. Sometimes they grossly overestimate how successful they have already been in increasing urgency. Sometimes they lack patience: "Enough with the preliminaries; let's get on with it." In many cases, executives become paralyzed by the downside possibilities. They worry that employees with seniority will become defensive, that morale will drop, that events will spin out of control, that short-term business results will be jeopardized, that the stock will sink, and that they will be blamed for creating a crisis.

A paralyzed senior management often comes from having too many managers and not enough leaders. Management's mandate is to minimize risk and to keep the current system operating. Change, by definition, requires creating a new system, which in turn always demands leadership. Phase one in a renewal process typically goes nowhere until enough real leaders are promoted or hired into senior-level jobs.

Transformations often begin, and begin well, when an organization has a new head who is a good leader and who sees the need for a major change. If the renewal target is the entire company, the CEO is key. If change is needed in a division, the division general manager is key. When these individuals are not new leaders, great leaders, or change champions, phase one can be a huge challenge.

Bad business results are both a blessing and a curse in the first phase. On the positive side, losing money does catch people's attention. But it also gives less maneuvering room. With good business results, the opposite is true: Convincing people of the need for change is much harder, but you have more resources to help make changes.

But whether the starting point is good performance or bad, in the more successful cases I have witnessed, an individual or a group always facilitates a frank discussion of potentially unpleasant facts about new competition, shrinking margins, decreasing market share, flat earnings, a lack of revenue growth, or other relevant indices of a declining competitive position. Because there seems to be an almost universal human tendency to shoot the bearer of bad news, especially if the head of the organization is not a change champion, executives in these companies often rely on outsiders to bring unwanted information. Wall Street analysts, customers, and consultants can all be helpful in this regard. The purpose of all this activity, in the words of one former CEO of a large European company, is "to make the status quo seem more dangerous than launching into the unknown."

In a few of the most successful cases, a group has manufactured a crisis. One CEO deliberately engineered the largest accounting loss in the company's history, creating huge pressures from Wall Street in the process. One division president commissioned first-ever customer satisfaction surveys, knowing full well that the results would be terrible. He then made these findings public. On the surface, such moves can look unduly risky. But there is also risk in playing it too safe: When the urgency rate is not pumped up enough, the transformation process cannot succeed, and the long-term future of the organization is put in jeopardy.

When is the urgency rate high enough? From what I have seen, the answer is when about 75% of a company's management is honestly convinced that business as usual is totally unacceptable. Anything less can produce very serious problems later on in the process.

Error 2: Not Creating a Powerful Enough Guiding Coalition

Major renewal programs often start with just one or two people. In cases of successful transformation efforts, the leadership coalition grows and grows over time. But whenever some minimum mass is not achieved early in the effort, nothing much worthwhile happens.

It is often said that major change is impossible unless the head of the organization is an active supporter. What I am talking about goes far beyond that. In successful transformations, the chairman or president or division general manager, plus another five or 15 or 50 people, come together and develop a shared commitment to excellent performance through renewal. In my experience, this group never includes all of the company's most senior executives because some people just won't buy in, at least not at first. But in the most successful cases, the coalition is always pretty powerful—in terms of titles, information and expertise, reputations, and relationships.

In both small and large organizations, a successful guiding team may consist of only three to five people during the first year of a renewal effort. But in big companies, the coalition needs to grow to the 20 to 50 range before much progress can be made in phase three and beyond. Senior managers always form the core of the group. But sometimes you find board members, a representative from a key customer, or even a powerful union leader.

Because the guiding coalition includes members who are not part of senior management, it tends to operate outside of the normal hierarchy by definition. This can be awkward, but it is clearly necessary. If the existing hierarchy were working well, there would be no need for a major transformation. But since the current system is not working, reform generally demands activity outside of formal boundaries, expectations, and protocol.

A high sense of urgency within the managerial ranks helps enormously in putting a guiding coalition together. But more is usually required. Someone needs to get these people together, help them develop a shared assessment of their company's problems and opportunities, and create a minimum level of trust and communication. Off-site retreats, for two or three days, are one popular vehicle for accomplishing this task. I have seen many groups of five to 35 executives attend a series of these retreats over a period of months.

Companies that fail in phase two usually underestimate the difficulties of producing change and thus the importance of a powerful guiding coalition. Sometimes they have no history of teamwork at the top and therefore undervalue the importance of this type of coalition. Sometimes they expect the team to be led by a staff executive from human resources, quality, or strategic planning instead of a key line manager. No matter how capable or dedicated the staff head, groups without strong line leadership never achieve the power that is required.

Efforts that don't have a powerful enough guiding coalition can make apparent progress for a while. But, sooner or later, the opposition gathers itself together and stops the change.

Error 3: Lacking a Vision

In every successful transformation effort that I have seen, the guiding coalition develops a picture of the future that is relatively easy to communicate and appeals to customers, stockholders, and employees. A vision always goes beyond the numbers that are typically found in five-year plans. A vision says something that helps clarify the direction in which an organization needs to move. Sometimes the first draft comes mostly from a single individual. It is usually a bit blurry, at least initially. But after the coalition works at it for three or five or even 12 months, something much better emerges through their tough analytical thinking and a little dreaming. Eventually, a strategy for achieving that vision is also developed.

In one midsize European company, the first pass at a vision contained two-thirds of the basic ideas that were in the final product. The concept of global reach was in the initial version from the beginning. So was the idea of becoming preeminent in certain businesses. But one central idea in the final version—getting out of low value-added activities—came only after a series of discussions over a period of several months.

Without a sensible vision, a transformation effort can easily dissolve into a list of confusing and incompatible projects that can take the organization in the wrong direction or nowhere at all. Without a sound vision, the reengineering project in the accounting department, the new 360-degree performance appraisal from the human resources department, the plant's quality program, the cultural change project in the sales force will not add up in a meaningful way.

In failed transformations, you often find plenty of plans, directives, and programs but no vision. In one case, a company gave out four-inch-thick notebooks describing its change effort. In mind-numbing detail, the books spelled out procedures, goals, methods, and deadlines. But nowhere was there a clear and compelling statement of where all this was leading. Not surprisingly, most of the employees with whom I talked were either confused or alienated. The big, thick books did not rally them together or inspire change. In fact, they probably had just the opposite effect.

In a few of the less successful cases that I have seen, management had a sense of direction, but it was too complicated or blurry to be useful. Recently, I asked an executive in a midsize company to describe his vision and received in return a barely comprehensible 30-minute lecture. Buried in his answer were the basic elements of a sound vision. But they were buried—deeply.

A useful rule of thumb: If you can't communicate the vision to someone in five minutes or less and get a reaction that signifies both understanding and interest, you are not yet done with this phase of the transformation process.

Error 4: Undercommunicating the Vision by a Factor of Ten

I've seen three patterns with respect to communication, all very common. In the first, a group actually does develop a pretty good transformation vision and then proceeds to communicate it by holding a single meeting or sending out a single communication. Having used about 0.0001% of the yearly intracompany communication, the group is startled when few people seem to understand the new approach. In the second pattern, the head of the organization spends a considerable amount of time making speeches to employee groups, but most people still don't get it (not surprising, since vision captures only 0.0005% of the total yearly communication). In the third pattern, much more effort goes into newsletters and speeches, but some very visible senior executives still behave in ways that are antithetical to the vision. The net result is that cynicism among the troops goes up, while belief in the communication goes down.

Transformation is impossible unless hundreds or thousands of people are willing to help, often to the point of making short-term sacrifices. Employees will not make sacrifices, even if they are unhappy with the status quo, unless they believe that useful change is possible. Without credible communication, and a lot of it, the hearts and minds of the troops are never captured.

This fourth phase is particularly challenging if the short-term sacrifices include job losses. Gaining understanding and support is tough when downsizing is a part of the vision. For this reason, successful visions usually include new growth possibilities and the commitment to treat fairly anyone who is laid off.

Executives who communicate well incorporate messages into their hour-by-hour activities. In a routine discussion about a business problem, they talk about how proposed solutions fit (or don't fit) into the bigger picture. In a regular performance appraisal, they talk about how the employee's behavior helps or undermines the vision. In a review of a division's quarterly performance, they talk not only about the numbers but also about how the division's executives are contributing to the transformation. In a routine Q&A with employees at a company facility, they tie their answers back to renewal goals.

In more successful transformation efforts, executives use all existing communication channels to broadcast the vision. They turn boring, unread company newsletters into lively articles about the vision. They take ritualistic, tedious quarterly management meetings and turn them into exciting discussions of the transformation.

They throw out much of the company's generic management education and replace it with courses that focus on business problems and the new vision. The guiding principle is simple: Use every possible channel, especially those that are being wasted on nonessential information.

Perhaps even more important, most of the executives I have known in successful cases of major change learn to "walk the talk." They consciously attempt to become a living symbol of the new corporate culture. This is often not easy. A 60-year-old plant manager who has spent precious little time over 40 years thinking about customers will not suddenly behave in a customer-oriented way. But I have witnessed just such a person change, and change a great deal. In that case, a high level of urgency helped. The fact that the man was a part of the guiding coalition and the vision-creation team also helped. So did all the communication, which kept reminding him of the desired behavior, and all the feedback from his peers and subordinates, which helped him see when he was not engaging in that behavior.

Communication comes in both words and deeds, and the latter are often the most powerful form. Nothing undermines change more than behavior by important individuals that is inconsistent with their words.

Error 5: Not Removing Obstacles to the New Vision

Successful transformations begin to involve large numbers of people as the process progresses. Employees are emboldened to try new approaches, to develop new ideas, and to provide leadership. The only constraint is that the actions fit within the broad parameters of the overall vision. The more people involved, the better the outcome.

To some degree, a guiding coalition empowers others to take action simply by successfully communicating the new direction. But communication is never sufficient by itself. Renewal also requires the removal of obstacles. Too often, an employee understands the new vision and wants to help make it happen, but an elephant appears to be blocking the path. In some cases, the elephant is in the person's head, and the challenge is to convince the individual that no external obstacle exists. But in most cases, the blockers are very real.

Sometimes the obstacle is the organizational structure: Narrow job categories can seriously undermine efforts to increase productivity or make it very difficult even to think about customers. Sometimes compensation or performance-appraisal systems make people choose between the new vision and their own self-interest. Perhaps worst of all are bosses who refuse to change and who make demands that are inconsistent with the overall effort.

One company began its transformation process with much publicity and actually made good progress through the fourth phase. Then the change effort ground to a halt because the officer in charge of the company's largest division was allowed to undermine most of the new initiatives. He paid lip service to the process but did not change his behavior or encourage his managers to change. He did not reward the unconventional ideas called for in the vision. He allowed human resource systems to remain intact even when they were clearly inconsistent with the new ideals. I think the officer's motives were complex. To some degree, he did not believe the company needed major change. To some degree, he felt personally threatened by all the change. To some degree, he was afraid that he could not produce both change and the expected operating profit. But despite the fact that they backed the renewal effort, the other officers did virtually nothing to stop the one blocker. Again, the reasons were complex. The company had no history of confronting problems like this. Some people were afraid of the officer. The CEO was concerned that he might lose a talented executive. The net result was disastrous. Lower-level managers concluded that senior management had lied to them about their commitment to renewal, cynicism grew, and the whole effort collapsed.

In the first half of a transformation, no organization has the momentum, power, or time to get rid of all obstacles. But the big ones must be confronted and removed. If the blocker is a person, it is important that he or she be treated fairly and in a way that is consistent with the new vision. Action is essential, both to empower others and to maintain the credibility of the change effort as a whole.

Error 6: Not Systematically Planning for, and Creating, Short-Term Wins

Real transformation takes time, and a renewal effort risks losing momentum if there are no short-term goals to meet and celebrate. Most people won't go on the long march unless they see compelling evidence in 12 to 24 months that the journey is producing expected results. Without short-term wins, too many people give up or actively join the ranks of those people who have been resisting change.

One to two years into a successful transformation effort, you find quality beginning to go up on certain indices or the decline in net income stopping. You find some successful new product introductions or an upward shift in market share. You find an impressive productivity improvement or a statistically higher customer satisfaction rating. But whatever the case, the win is unambiguous. The result is not just a judgment call that can be discounted by those opposing change.

Creating short-term wins is different from hoping for short-term wins. The latter is passive, the former active. In a successful transformation, managers actively look for ways to obtain clear performance improvements, establish goals in the yearly planning system, achieve the objectives, and reward the people involved with recognition, promotions, and even money. For example, the guiding coalition at a U.S. manufacturing company produced a highly visible and successful new product introduction about 20 months after the start of its renewal effort. The new product was selected about six months into the effort because it met multiple criteria: It could be designed and launched in a relatively short period, it could be handled by a small team of people who were devoted to the new vision, it had upside potential, and the new product-development team could operate outside the established departmental structure without practical problems. Little was left to chance, and the win boosted the credibility of the renewal process.

Managers often complain about being forced to produce short-term wins, but I've found that pressure can be a useful element in a change effort. When it becomes clear to people that major change will take a long time, urgency levels can drop. Commitments to produce short-term wins help keep the urgency level up and force detailed analytical thinking that can clarify or revise visions.

Error 7: Declaring Victory Too Soon

After a few years of hard work, managers may be tempted to declare victory with the first clear performance improvement. While celebrating a win is fine, declaring the war won can be catastrophic. Until changes sink deeply into a company's culture, a process that can take five to ten years, new approaches are fragile and subject to regression.

In the recent past, I have watched a dozen change efforts operate under the reengineering theme. In all but two cases, victory was declared and the expensive consultants were paid and thanked when the first major project was completed after two to three years. Within two more years, the useful changes that had been introduced slowly disappeared. In two of the ten cases, it's hard to find any trace of the reengineering work today.

Over the past 20 years, I've seen the same sort of thing happen to huge quality projects, organizational development efforts, and more. Typically, the problems start early in the process: The urgency level is not intense enough, the guiding coalition is not powerful enough, and the vision is not clear enough. But it is the premature victory celebration that kills momentum. And then the powerful forces associated with tradition take over.

Ironically, it is often a combination of change initiators and change resistors that creates the premature victory celebration. In their enthusiasm over a clear sign of progress, the initiators go overboard. They are then joined by resistors, who are quick to spot any opportunity to stop change. After the celebration is over, the resistors point to the victory as a sign that the war has been won and the troops should be sent home. Weary troops allow themselves to be convinced that they won. Once home, the foot soldiers are reluctant to climb back on the ships. Soon thereafter, change comes to a halt, and tradition creeps back in.

Instead of declaring victory, leaders of successful efforts use the credibility afforded by short-term wins to tackle even bigger problems. They go after systems and structures that are not consistent with the transformation vision and have not been confronted before. They pay great attention to who is promoted, who is hired, and how people are developed. They include new reengineering projects that are even bigger in scope than the initial ones. They understand that renewal efforts take not months but years. In fact, in one of the most successful transformations that I have ever seen, we quantified the amount of change that occurred each year over a seven-year period. On a scale of one (low) to ten (high), year one received a two, year two a four, year three a three, year four a seven, year five an eight, year six a four, and year seven a two. The peak came in year five, fully 36 months after the first set of visible wins.

Error 8: Not Anchoring Changes in the Corporation's Culture

In the final analysis, change sticks when it becomes "the way we do things around here," when it seeps into the bloodstream of the corporate body. Until new behaviors are rooted in social norms and shared values, they are subject to degradation as soon as the pressure for change is removed.

Two factors are particularly important in institutionalizing change in corporate culture. The first is a conscious attempt to show people how the new approaches, behaviors, and attitudes have helped improve performance. When people are left on their own to make the connections, they sometimes create very inaccurate links. For example, because results improved while charismatic Harry was boss, the troops link his mostly idiosyncratic style with those results instead of seeing how their own improved customer service and productivity were instrumental. Helping people see the right connections requires communication. Indeed, one company was relentless, and it paid off enormously. Time was spent at every major management meeting to discuss why performance was increasing. The company newspaper ran article after article showing how changes had boosted earnings.

The second factor is taking sufficient time to make sure that the next generation of top management really does personify the new approach. If the requirements for promotion don't change, renewal rarely lasts. One bad succession decision at the top of an organization can undermine a decade of hard work. Poor succession decisions are possible when boards of directors are not an integral part of the renewal effort. In at least three instances I have seen, the champion for change was the retiring executive, and although his successor was not a resistor, he was not a change champion. Because the boards did not understand the transformations in any detail, they could not see that their choices were not good fits. The retiring executive in one case tried unsuccessfully to talk his board into a less seasoned candidate who better personified the transformation. In the other two cases, the CEOs did not resist the boards' choices, because they felt the transformation could not be undone by their successors. They were wrong. Within two years, signs of renewal began to disappear at both companies.

THERE ARE STILL MORE MISTAKES that people make, but these eight are the big ones. I realize that in a short article everything is made to sound a bit too simplistic. In reality, even successful change efforts are messy and full of surprises. But just as a relatively simple vision is needed to guide people through a major change, so a vision of the change process can reduce the error rate. And fewer errors can spell the difference between success and failure.

Originally published in January 2007
Reprint R0701J; HBR OnPoint 1710

Eight Steps to Transforming Your Organization

1 Establishing a Sense of Urgency

- Examining market and competitive realities
- Identifying and discussing crises, potential crises, or major opportunities

2 Forming a Powerful Guiding Coalition

- Assembling a group with enough power to lead the change effort
- Encouraging the group to work together as a team

3 Creating a Vision

- Creating a vision to help direct the change effort
- Developing strategies for achieving that vision

4 Communicating the Vision

- Using every vehicle possible to communicate the new vision and strategies
- Teaching new behaviors by the example of the guiding coalition

5 Empowering Others to Act on the Vision

- Getting rid of obstacles to change
- Changing systems or structures that seriously undermine the vision
- Encouraging risk taking and nontraditional ideas, activities, and actions

6 Planning for and Creating Short-Term Wins

- Planning for visible performance improvements
- Creating those improvements
- Recognizing and rewarding employees involved in the improvements

7 Consolidating Improvements and Producing Still More Change

- Using increased credibility to change systems, structures, and policies that don't fit the vision
- Hiring, promoting, and developing employees who can implement the vision
- Reinvigorating the process with new projects, themes, and change agents

8 Institutionalizing New Approaches

- Articulating the connections between the new behaviors and corporate success
- Developing the means to ensure leadership development and succession

About the Contributors

DULEEP ALUWIHARE is the managing partner at the accounting firm Ernst & Young in Warsaw, Poland.

ALEXANDER B. CUMMINGS is the president and chief operating officer of the Coca-Cola Company's Africa Group. He is based in Windsor, UK.

JOHN J. GABARRO is the UPS Foundation Professor of Human Resource Management in Organizational Behavior at Harvard Business School in Boston.

ARTHUR GENSLER founded Gensler—a global architecture, design, planning, and consulting firm—41 years ago. The firm has grown to 2,400 people in 30 offices.

LINDA A. HILL is the Wallace Brett Donham Professor of Business Administration at Harvard Business School in Boston.

FRANZ HUMER is the chairman and CEO of the pharmaceutical firm Roche, based in Basel, Switzerland.

MARK HUNTER is an investigative journalist and an adjunct professor of communications at Insead in Fontainebleau, France.

HERMINIA IBARRA is the Insead Chaired Professor of Organizational Behavior at Insead in Fontainebleau, France, where she also directs the Leadership Transition, an executive program for managers moving into broader leadership roles.

GARY JACKSON is the president of Blackwater USA, a private military contractor and security firm based in Moyock, North Carolina.

OLLI-PEKKA KALLASVUO has been the president and CEO of the telecommunications company Nokia, in Espoo, Finland, since June 2006.

ROBERT S. KAPLAN is the former vice chairman of the Goldman Sachs Group and is the Thomas S. Murphy Senior Lecturer of Business Administration at Harvard Business School in Boston.

ALAN KLAPMEIER cofounded Cirrus Design, a Duluth, Minnesota–based manufacturer of private aircraft, with his brother, Dale, in 1984.

JOHN P. KOTTER, now retired, was the Konosuke Matsushita Professor of Leadership at Harvard Business School in Boston.

DAVID A. NADLER is the chairman of New York–based Mercer Delta Consulting, a global management consulting firm that specializes in executive leadership, organizational change, and corporate governance.

SERGEY PETROV is the founder and sole owner of the $2.4 billion Rolf Group, Russia's largest foreign car importer and distributor.

KATHLEEN K. REARDON is a professor of management and organization at the University of Southern California Marshall School of Business.

Index

DEC 5 2007